EXHALE

EXHALE

Chanda Fulgium

Copyright © 2020 by Chanda Fulgium.

Library of Congress Control Number: 2020903464
ISBN: Hardcover 978-1-7960-8806-9
Softcover 978-1-7960-8805-2
eBook 978-1-7960-8804-5

All rights reserved. No part of this book may be reproduced or transmitted in any form or by any means, electronic or mechanical, including photocopying, recording, or by any information storage and retrieval system, without permission in writing from the copyright owner.

This is a work of fiction. Names, characters, places and incidents either are the product of the author's imagination or are used fictitiously, and any resemblance to any actual persons, living or dead, events, or locales is entirely coincidental.

Any people depicted in stock imagery provided by Getty Images are models, and such images are being used for illustrative purposes only.
Certain stock imagery © Getty Images.

NKJV – New King James Version
Scripture taken from the New King James Version. Copyright 1979, 1980, 1982 by Thomas Nelson, inc. Used by permission. All rights reserved.

Scripture quotations marked TPT are from The Passion Translation®. Copyright © 2017, 2018 by Passion & Fire Ministries, Inc. Used by permission. All rights reserved. ThePassionTranslation.com.

All Scripture quotations are from The Passion Translation®. Copyright © 2017, 2018 by Passion & Fire Ministries, Inc. Used by permission. All rights reserved. ThePassionTranslation.com.

All Scripture quotations are taken from THE MESSAGE, copyright © 1993, 2002, 2018 by Eugene H. Peterson. Used by permission of NavPress. All rights reserved. Represented by Tyndale House Publishers, Inc.

Unless otherwise indicated, all Scripture quotations are taken from THE MESSAGE, copyright © 1993, 2002, 2018 by Eugene H. Peterson. Used by permission of NavPress. All rights reserved. Represented by Tyndale House Publishers, Inc.

Scripture quotations marked MSG are taken from THE MESSAGE, copyright © 1993, 2002, 2018 by Eugene H. Peterson. Used by permission of NavPress. All rights reserved. Represented by Tyndale House Publishers, Inc.

Print information available on the last page.

Rev. date: 02/22/2020

To order additional copies of this book, contact:
Xlibris
1-888-795-4274
www.Xlibris.com
Orders@Xlibris.com
809629

TABLE OF CONTENTS

Foreword vii
Endorsements ix
Acknowledgments xv

Beat to Your Own Drum 1
Beautifully Broken—His Masterpiece 5
Beauty for Ashes 9
Choose Faith—Even When You Are Afraid 13
Dancing Through the Fire 16
Don't Settle—His Best Is on the Way 20
Fill Me Up, God! 23
He Knows My Name 26
How Bad Do You Want It? 30
Imperfectly Perfect 34
In His Presence 37
Jesus, Have Your Way 40
Legacy 43
Lies and Timelines 47
Live in the Present—Enjoy the Process 51
Look Like Jesus—In Your Unique Expression 55
Love the One in Front of You 58
More than Enough—In Him 62
On My Knees in the Midst of the Storm 65
Our Response in the Waiting 69
Out of These Ashes—Hope Will Arise 73
Seeing Him in Everyday Life 77
Sharing What He Has Done in Our Lives 81

So Thankful—The Right Perspective 85
Take a Moment 88
Take One Step 92
The Faith of a Child 96
The Great Exchange 100
The Power of Listening 104
Wisdom to Make Great Choices.. 108
You Are My Hiding Place 111
You Are So Loved 115

About the Author 119

Foreword

I urge any woman business leader, mother, or hungry daughter of God to read *Exhale*. I pray you will weigh and embrace the spirit, truth, and heartbeat of Chanda Fulgium displayed on the pages of this book. Chanda is raw, real, and inspiring. God can work with a transparent humble heart. He loves a person whose heart is turned toward Him. This is Chanda.

Chanda and I found each other in 2009 as we both ministered to the broken-hearted. A lifelong friendship of loving God and loving others was formed. Since then, we have partnered together in global speaking to women and business leaders. Her positive outlook on life based on love for God and His word is irresistible and life giving.

Exhale is a devotional guide to encourage brave women who are breaking through the struggles of ordinary life, the broken places of our past, and through the daily pressures of being a strong Christian woman leader in a worldly high-pressure world. If you need an anchor in life's storm, good news to encourage your day, or a reminder of who God says you are, you will love the balance and wisdom of this book!

Judy Capps
Founder/President
Hope of Northeast Texas
www.hopeofnet.org

Endorsements

Chanda Fulgium's devotionals are inspiring, comforting, and relevant to daily life. I look forward every day to the next one. They speak to my heart, show me true hope, and make me lean in with gratitude each and every day. Each one speaks to me on such a personal level, it is truly amazing how her words and teaching can feel so "tailored" to me.

I am relatively new to studying the Bible, her devotionals are Scripture-based. They propel me to study further on the Word. They give me strength, force me to expand my introspection and speak to my heart. Her thought-provoking style and words of encouragement combine to create devotionals that can truly change lives every, single day.

Connie King
COO – Willis Senior Housecalls

Reading Chanda's devotional book was like a trip to heaven. The Holy Spirit was present, tears flowed from my eyes, and my heart was beating wildly. Chanda was definitely used by God through this devotional to minister to our hearts. If you want an additional dose of Faith, Hope and Love from Heavenly Father, read this book. Chanda is a woman of God who has gone through very difficult times, but who chose to grab the Lord and serve Him. She has impacted people through her powerful conferences all over the world and has experienced his amazing mercy on her and her adorable children.
Ingrid Martinez
Owner and Executive Director of Unique Management Solutions, HR Consulting Firm, Dominican Republic
Colaborator of Global Advance, Dominican Republic
Leader Couples Ministry Iglesia Cristina, Dominican Republic

With every breath of my being, I know Jesus has an amazing plan for my life. I know this and yet I wake up with a sigh as go through my Christian routine. Then I read *Exhale* to supplement my Christian routine. This book stirred my holy spirit, it broke me and allowed me to be raw and unfiltered with God. I found myself wanting to "cheat" and read more than one devotional per day. In a short period, I drew closer to Jesus, to hear Jesus, to rest in Jesus and finally to dance with Jesus.

The author, Chanda Fulgium, is God's communication vessel to all women and men that know Jesus but also know there is more. Pick up the book- Inhale this daily word and *Exhale* while you dance in the fire with The Saviour.

Fonda Ivy BS, MS, SPHR
Economist

Exhale by Chanda Fulgium is a true colored photograph with no filters of what we as Christians live today in the midst of fast paced, high demand, challenging times. Reading throughout the devotional, as a mother, wife and corporate executive, I can relate to many moments of frustration, desperation, impatience and my own lack of memory to recall the numerous times our Lord has answered prayers, bringing light out of darkness, hope out of ashes in miraculous and unexpected ways.

Exhale reminds me that **I need to breathe**, you need to breathe. Yes indeed, we all need to breathe, and live out a bold faith that will make us not stronger in our own strength but indeed stronger in Him. *Exhale* is a breath of fresh air that provides me a realistic yet divine perspective of my constant need and dependence of our loving Father. I can clearly hear his voice in her journey on how our loving heavenly Father desires we enjoy the process, enjoy the journey for his higher plans to be unfolded. Chanda, thank you so much for leading me into a new stage of exhalation for Gods purpose and glory.

I pray many more women receive the gift of exhaling and truly resting - depending on our Lord every day.

With love,
Karina Cruz
Servant of God
Wife, Mother, Daughter
Corporate Affairs and Communications Executive

As a leader and speaker, Chanda has connected with audiences worldwide through her willingness to approach life's challenges with vulnerable humility and unwavering faith. Exhale by Chanda Fulgium is a much-needed invitation to rest from the fast-paced world around us: to rest in the sovereignty of God, in the truth of His Word, and in His unchanging love. If you're in a season of waiting, exhausted in well-doing, struggling with fear, or battling disappointment, you'll find great comfort in these pages. Chanda's personal life stories will welcome you in like a compassionate friend, but it's God's promises in Scripture woven throughout that will help redirect your heart to the peace, hope, and joy that can only be found in Him.

Whitney Daugherty
Global Advance – Esther Initiative

With the turning of each page, you will find the desire to not only inhale, but genuinely *Exhale* through Chanda's relatable stories and incredible insights that leave you craving more of Jesus while becoming increasingly victorious. Like Joshua, the author encourages us to fight our battles in very specific and tangible ways, with courage. This engaging compilation gives you an opportunity to pause and regain exhilarating strength while letting go of the past. *Exhale* is essential to emerge edified and be highly effective for such a time as this each day.

Sherry Chester, TWBC Children's Pastor
Leadership & People Developer
Author of *Viction*
sherry-chester.com

Chanda Fulgium is emerging as a fresh voice in the business and ministry world. Her work of devotions touches the very root of our everyday life in a personal and raw way. A single mother, a business executive, an anointed prophetic evangelist, she speaks from deep experience and love for people. Her style of taking the reader from Chanda's story to the reader's life allows the reader to experience growth with each devotion. There are many devotions on the market today, but what marks this one is a prophetic relevancy that can be life changing for a reader. Chanda's heart captures our heart in a way that leads us to greater intimacy with our creator in a unique & contemporary way!

Suzy Moffatt
Retired School Teacher

Chanda is one of my dearest friends. We met seven years ago on a soccer field and immediately knew we had a connection. We are both single mothers doing our best to balance parenting, work, personal well-being, and most importantly living life for Jesus. Chanda has been a huge inspiration to me. Her journey, hard- work, dedication and "never give up" attitude has ministered to me on so many levels.

Chanda has taught me that by obedience and faithfulness, God will always provide. Her knowledge of God's word comes from years obedient time in his word, seeking him in prayer, devotion and praise! Her compassion, empathy and past experiences allow her to minister to other women. She is an advocate of SMART goals and never makes excuses. She lives by example in all that she does and has taught me how to set a goal, follow through with my actions and accomplish it!

Chanda loves people right where they're at. She never judges or condemns. She is an encourager and advocate of trusting by faith, following God's word and living the life God has planned for her. I am so thankful to be living life with Chanda. She is truly a Woman of God and I'm excited for this part of her journey and the people that will hear God's word through her.

Nichole Anguiano RD, LD
(Registered and Licensed Dietitian)

Exhale is a very realistic journey of the testimony and truth shared by the author through the eyes of experience in a personal and actionable revelation. In this devotional, you will find relatable life experiences aligned with the Word of God leaving you freshly inspired to pursue and cultivate a deeper walk with the Father. An amazing invitation to activate truth and transformation as the Holy Spirit leads us to live a life full of purpose and authenticity.

Having known Chanda Fulgium for over 15 years, I have witnessed her incredible love for the LORD and whole heart's desire to spread the Gospel around the world. Using the multitude of gifts that God has given her, she is impacting the Kingdom. Each devotional has been strategically lined out for His glory.

Kristi Brewer
Realtor at Coldwell Banker Apex. Realtors

I was privileged to be Chanda's pastor for several years. As a church member, she was faithful, helpful, and always encouraging. Someone told me she was an executive, and she helped lead a cooperate team. I found out she taught her team leadership skills. I seized the opportunity, and I asked her to conduct a leadership seminar for our church and the community. I also had her speak to our congregation. It was a tremendous success.

What I discovered is Chanda is a walking leadership manual. She teaches you how to lead yourself well, and she inspires you to lead others with humility and excellence. Chanda is also an inspirational communicator. The lady can preach! She is very knowledgeable of the Scriptures.

What many do not know about Chanda's success in her career came from extremely hard work, while being a single parent. Her book will inspire you, encourage you, challenge you, and equip you. I believe it will build your faith to overcome. Enjoy!

Dr. Terry Sparks
Peace to the Nations

Acknowledgments

Thank you to Elijah and Joshua, the most amazing young men in the universe, my beauty for ashes, and Mrs. Miriam—I cannot imagine living life without you.
To my amazing mentors, friends, and family, who poked the bear and helped this gift come out of hibernation.
To Jesus Christ, the Love of my life.

Beat to Your Own Drum

There's elegance in all You create
Your grand designs leave us amazed
The wonders of the way we've been made
Speak of Your power, tell of Your grace
So what am I going to do with this life You gave me?
What could I do but live for Your praise

—Matt Redman, "Fearfully and Wonderfully Made"

I was sitting in the nail salon, having my nails done. Don't start it because it's an expensive and time-consuming habit! The ambiance was a semispa experience with fountains flowing, classical music playing, and chandeliers hanging from the ceiling. Over in the corner, a woman was jamming to faster and happier beats through her AirPods. She was dancing to the rhythm of a much different tune—doing her own thing.

At first, it was odd. Compared to the atmosphere and other people around her, she stood out like red paint on a white canvas. Then it was hysterical. She kept catching my eye, completely oblivious to me or anyone else watching her.

It reminded me of the weekend before when I was driving my youngest son and four of his friends to a futsal game. My oldest son was in the front seat with me. I was singing at a reasonable volume to the worship music playing on the radio. I could feel him glaring at me. I would never do this if it were a car full of his friends because he would be completely mortified. He is fourteen, and EVERYTHING embarrasses him. (He once asked me to drop him off in a ditch at a birthday party versus driving up the driveway. I pointed out that he looked far more ridiculous emerging from the ditch.)

When I knew he could hold his tongue no longer (this challenge runs in our family), my youngest son started belting out the same song at maximum Joshua volume. I busted out laughing because he ultimately does not care what anyone thinks.

I was listening to Pastor Bryan Sparks speak today on working the gifts and talents God gave you, and he talked about how he would listen to all these famous pastors on podcasts to teach him how to be better at speaking and preaching. At some point, God told him, "I have called you to be uniquely you versus an echo of someone else." This statement arrested my attention and fully resonated with me.

We should learn from others around us. Equally, it is vitally important to be who He has called us to be versus an imitation of someone else's calling. We often focus on the things we don't like about ourselves versus the things that we do like—those things that make us unique and wonderful.

My oldest son is continually trying to gain weight. He eats more than the rest of us put together. On the other hand, I am always trying to lose weight. Straight-haired people wish they had curly hair. Those of us with curly hair use a tremendous amount of product and straightening irons to calm our wild heads of hair. We look at others, and we wish we had their lives or their gifts. We doubt ourselves while others are looking at us, wishing they had our lives and our set of talents.

God was and is so intentional about the way He made us. He intentionally gifted me as a mouthpiece for the Kingdom of God through voice and the written word. He gave me a strong personality that He could mold into leadership. He gave me the gift of encouraging and motivating other people into their destinies. Likewise, He gave you a calling, a purpose, a unique gift set, and a way of thinking that brings a solution and a connection to a group of people that only you can bring.

My prayer today is that you embrace the "you" He made you to be. Trust Him to take what you are willing to give Him, and He will do something amazing through you. See a need and be the solution. Just say yes and do what He tells you to do.

> *You formed my innermost being, shaping my delicate inside and my intricate outside, and wove them all together in my mother's womb. ¹⁴ I thank you, God, for making me so mysteriously complex! Everything you do is marvelously breathtaking. It simply amazes me to think about it! How thoroughly you know me, Lord! ¹⁵ You even formed every bone in my body when you created me in the secret place, carefully, skillfully shaping me from nothing to something. ¹⁶ You saw who you created me to be before I became me! Before I'd ever seen the light of day, the number of days you planned for me were already recorded in your book.* (Ps. 139:13–16)

Questions:

1. What are the qualities that make you unique? Have you ever tried to hide those unique qualities or become someone else to fit in better in relationships and peer groups? What are some ways you can celebrate the way God made you? How can you leverage the attributes that make you you?

2. How do you help others to be authentic when they are around you?

3. What gifts and talents do you have that you can surrender to Jesus? What are some ways He can use you in this place? Are there some areas He is asking you to step forward? How will you say yes?

Beautifully Broken—His Masterpiece

> When I thought I'd lost me,
> You knew where I'd left me
> You reintroduced me to Your love
> You picked up all my pieces,
> Put me back together
> You are the Defender of my heart.
>
> —Rita Springer, "Defender"

When God asked me to start writing again, I came to the negotiation table with Him. I am usually quick to obey, but I sometimes like to set my own terms. I don't know what to say, so YOU will have to flow through me. I don't want to talk about that because it makes me too raw and vulnerable, simultaneously in the writing venue and life. I can't wait to share those Jerry Springer moments from my life, said NO ONE EVER.

People are saved by the blood of the lamb and the power of the testimony. Bill Johnson once stated, "When you share your testimony, it releases the DNA for God to do it again." The reality is we have all done pieces of stupid in our lives. However, many people have trouble moving forward at full capacity. They choose to stay in their past for the rest of their future.

I remember climbing out of a rebellious phase in my life and relegating myself to the back row of the church. I knew I needed to be in the Presence of God and with His people, but I would never resume a leadership or teaching position again. I did not deserve it. I was not and would never be good enough again—as if I was ever good enough to carry the call and anointing He placed on my life.

I knew His Word said His gifts and callings were without repentance, and yet I could not get past not being worthy and not being enough. I was reading a book titled *The Call* by Rick Joyner. I was startled when I read about thinking that your situation was too much for the blood of Jesus. He compared it to slapping God in the face and negating the Cross completely—where He sacrificed His only Son that you could live life abundantly. WWHHAATT!

My fall from grace was not a surprise to Him. He was not on a coffee break: "What, Chanda made some mistakes? Oh wow, we are going to have to rewrite the history of the universe now. She will have to go to Plan B!" He knew my choices before I made them.

I remember my son had lost his privileges because of an attitude and poorly spoken words. He kept asking me, "How long?" I wanted to reinstate those privileges, but I knew I needed to see a true heart change because his character was at stake. In that same breath, Holy Spirit whispered in my heart, "The same goes for you—I can't wait to reinstate you. The moment your heart is right and repentance (true 180 heart change), we move forward."

His love is not conditional. His grace is sufficient. His mercies are new every day. There is no plan B for your life, and your gifts and callings don't change when you make a mistake. There is a cost and often consequences for sin and mistakes, but God IS faithful. There is NOTHING that can separate you from His love. There is nothing SO BIG that He cannot walk you through to the other side. He will pick up your broken pieces, put you back together—even more beautifully than before your mess. You ARE His masterpiece, and He is always at work in and for you.

> *Through the Lord's mercies we are not consumed,*
> *Because His compassions fail not.*
> *23 They are new every morning;*
> *Great is Your faithfulness.*
> *24 "The Lord is my portion," says my soul,*
> *"Therefore, I hope in Him!"* (Lam. 3:22–24)

For the gifts and the calling of God are irrevocable. 30 For as you were once disobedient to God, yet have now obtained mercy through their disobedience, 31 even so these also have now been disobedient, that through the mercy shown you they also may obtain mercy. (Rom. 11:29–31)

For I am persuaded that neither death nor life, nor angels nor principalities nor powers, nor things present nor things to come, 39 nor height nor depth, nor any other created thing, shall be able to separate us from the love of God which is in Christ Jesus our Lord. (Rom. 8:38–39)

Questions:

1. How do you handle past mistakes? Are they holding you back from your present and your future? Do you continue to try and punish yourself, or are you ready to put it behind you? Are there some places where you need to forgive yourself?

2. Are there some areas in your life where you have settled for plan B? Do you have dreams you have put on the shelf? What are some steps you can take to resume plan A and go after your dreams?

3. Are there some places you can share your testimony to make a difference in someone else's life?

Beauty for Ashes

In the waiting, in the searching
In the healing and the hurting
Like a blessing buried in the broken pieces
Every minute, every moment
Where I've been and where I'm going
Even when I didn't know it or couldn't see it.

—Zach Williams and Dolly Parton, "There Was Jesus"

Staring out along the Amalfi Coast in Positano, Italy, my breath was completely taken away at the beauty surrounding me. I was praying and walking up the steep inclines. I was worshipping God for His goodness. I heard Him say, "Taste and see that I AM good. See the majesty of My hand. I AM ABLE to do exceedingly and abundantly ABOVE anything you could ever ask for, think of or even imagine."

I remember dipping my toe in the waters of dating a few years ago. For the record, no one should have to date in their late thirties and early forties. Side note: this could be a one-woman stand-up comedy in multiple acts.

As I evolved into a professional first-date dater (I am sure this is grammatically incorrect, but you get the point), I thought, I need a life. I am entirely uninteresting. Who wants to talk about the deep things of God, my children, or wound care? I remember wishing I could travel so I would at least have some experiences to talk about on these first dates. Second dates would be the next goal I would tackle—at some point.

God answered my prayer in such a mighty way, and I saw myself in eleven different countries over the past five years for mission work,

work, and pleasure. I evolved from a woman who worked three jobs to pay her bills, barely, to a woman who is now a little more interesting. Now I am in a position to help others, and this is how extravagantly good my God IS.

I am completely in awe of what He has done in my life and the lives of those in my spheres of influence. He has delivered me from abuse, fear, poverty, and every lacking thing to wholeness, freedom, and abundance. He is ABLE and WILLING. What He has done for me, He will do for you. He is no respecter of persons. He IS the same God yesterday, today, and forever. He wants to see you living and walking in the fullness and PROMISES of everything He has for you and yours.

I am thankful for every stone of remembrance. I praise Him for beauty for my ashes. I am grateful—even for the hard things. They make me who I am today—a mosaic of strength and weakness, confidence, and humility, grit, and beauty. I am still in His process, and I continue to be transformed on a daily basis. I am grateful for his new mercies every day and His MORE THAN ENOUGH amazing grace.

I pray you see through His eyes the plans and purposes He has over your life. I pray you recognize how interesting you are to Him. Hand him the pieces of your broken heart and life; submit and surrender to His process. Let His love wash over you in waves. Allow the Master Potter to mold you into something beautiful. He is waiting on you.

> *The Spirit of the Lord God is upon Me,*
> *Because the Lord has anointed Me*
> *To preach good tidings to the poor;*
> *He has sent Me to heal the brokenhearted,*
> *To proclaim liberty to the captives,*
> *And the opening of the prison to those who are bound;*
> *2 To proclaim the acceptable year of the Lord,*
> *And the day of vengeance of our God;*
> *To comfort all who mourn,*
> *3 To [console those who mourn in Zion,*
> *To give them beauty for ashes,*

*The oil of joy for mourning,
The garment of praise for the spirit of heaviness;
That they may be called trees of righteousness,
The planting of the Lord, that He may be glorified.* (Isa. 61:1–3)

Questions:

1. What are some areas in your life where God has taken things and worked them together for your good? Where do you see the goodness of God in your life?

2. What are some areas where you would like to walk more fully in the Promises God has for you? List them out. Attach a Scripture to it. Begin to pray and declare His Word over your prayer list and note when you see it come to pass.

3. What are some broken pieces you need to hand over to Him? List them here and begin to pray and trust Him to put you back together again.

Choose Faith—Even When You Are Afraid

When David faced Goliath,
He didn't talk about how dangerous Goliath was.
He talked about how great God is.
Don't talk fear. Talk Faith.

—*I'm So Blessed Daily*

When we moved into our new neighborhood, my large white husky-German shepherd mix dog escaped the backyard during move in, and he bit our neighbor's dachshund on its backside. Yes, welcome to the neighborhood. Did I mention the neighbor is the head of the HOA too? Awesome, sigh. When Animal Control came to visit with Journey and me. He said, "If your dog had wanted to kill the neighbor's dog, he would have. He's just a bully."

While his assessment was not helpful to my neighbor (we are friends now, and he affectionately, somewhat, calls my dog Killer), it did not change our fear of it happening again. Likewise, it did not prevent us from facing the consequences of losing our dog (and worse, him hurting someone else's dog).

It reminds me of someone else we all contend with on a daily basis. The enemy only has lies that create fear to hold you back and keep you from everything you are called to be. I've heard it said this way, "Everything you have ever wanted is on the other side of fear and obedience."

I remember my journey coming out of an abusive marriage, where I had lived in fear for years. Fear of him hurting us. Fear of things always being this way. Fear of my children growing up in this environment. Fear of not being able to make it if I walked away.

And once I walked away, his voice on the answering machine, a text, a knock at the door still carried the power to paralyze me in that fear. Every time that fear kicked into gear, I would tell myself to breathe. I would start saying His Word out loud: "Greater is He Who is in me than he who is in this world. The LORD is my Light and Salvation; whom shall I fear? Yea though I walk through the valley of the shadow of death, I fear no evil: for You are with me; Your rod and Your staff, they comfort me. Fear not . . . for I AM with you. Be strong and courageous because I AM with you."

I took that step of obedience out of that situation, and God has been with us every step of the way. He has brought us out of poverty and into a place we can generously help others. He has healed all the broken and fearful places and brought us into a place of wholeness and choosing to do it afraid.

The enemy is a bully. He only has the power that you give him. I pray you would have a revelation of how much God loves you and is for you so you no longer have to be afraid. I pray today that you would breathe, declare God's powerful Word over your situation, and take that step of obedience—even when you feel afraid.

> *For God has not given us a spirit of fear, but of power and of love and of a sound mind. (2 Tim. 1:7)*
>
> *Don't panic. I AM with you. There's no need to fear for I AM your God. I will give you strength. I will help you. I will hold you steady, keep a firm grip on you. (Isa. 41:10)*
>
> *Be strong. Take courage. Don't be intimidated. Don't give them a second thought because God, your God, is striding ahead of you. He's right there with you. He won't let you down; He won't leave you. (Deut. 31:6)*

Questions:

1. What are some lies the enemy has been telling you? Where are the places you are experiencing fear? What Scriptures and Promises can you put in its place to reprogram your mind to think of what God says about you and your situation?

2. Are there some places where you need to be obedient to what God has asked of you? What was the last thing He asked you to do? What action steps can you take to move in His direction?

Dancing Through the Fire

> There was another in the fire
> Standing next to me
> There was another in the waters
> Holding back the seas
> And should I ever need reminding
> Of how I've been set free
> There is a cross that bears the burden
> Where another died for me
> There is another in the fire.
>
> —Hillsong, "Another in the Fire"

I had a friend once invite me on an eighteen-day canoe trip with no cell service, and we would camp on the ground by the river at night. I was like, do you know me? Find me some strategic Hiltons along the way, and we can discuss this like rational human beings. Don't judge. People at the Hilton need Jesus too, and I openly volunteer for this one.

Christian sayings like "We never lose because we work from a place of victory," "God's love never fails us," and "He died to give us life more abundantly" are super encouraging—until you are in the valley of the shadow of death or walking through fire. Then there is the chasm of seeing the words, but not knowing how to allow those words to live in you. How do I cross this river or climb this mountain to have those words be alive in my life?

What does grace under fire even look like? I look at the lives of amazing missionaries like Heidi Baker, who have endured tremendous tragedy to be able to walk in the level of triumph they experience today. Do I want to pay that price? I am honest enough to think on this before sputtering out an answer.

I remember when the boys were little and I had been without sleep for a REALLY LONG TIME (parents of infants and toddlers who never sleep can identify with me). I had moved them to a different bed, changed the sheets, and was whining my best and most pitiful prayer possible.

"I can't do this. You ask too much of me. Where are you? Did You forget about me?" I heard Him say, "Put your big-girl pants on. We have too much to do to sit here in this place. Did you, or did you not say yes?"

Let's define yes. I do remember multiple times in worship with arms reaching to heaven, saying, "Yes, LORD, I will do ANYTHING. USE ME, LORD. Let me be a conduit of your love and power to those around me. You can send me anywhere to do anything, and I say YES, LORD."

Okay, yes, I did say that. But You left out some major details. I may have rethought my response. Do I get to change my mind now that I know? Would I truly change my mind?

Twelve years later, as I walk through yet another fire, I am afraid. And it deceptively seems easier to stay paralyzed than to take that step forward into the heat. Yet I know I wouldn't trade all the victories, all the lives changed, all the miracles I have seen and experienced. I wouldn't exchange any of them for the misery of complacency and a life not lived.

This fire seems bigger, but it's because I don't recognize how much You have grown me. The fire seems scarier because it's on this side of triumph versus the other side. I can't do this without You, Jesus, but when YOU walk in the fire with me, I can do ALL things through YOU Who strengthens me. I don't have all the answers yet, but YOU have always been faithful. You have never let me down. You continue to wrap me in YOUR peace and love that passes all understanding. Tears may collect in the corners of my eyes as I face the unknown. Yet I look to the Heavens, and I know that You have asked for this dance. May we dance in the fire? My smile turns toward You. You have me, and You will never let me go. Grace, in the form of my rescuer and defender, walks with me and carries me through to the other side.

It's settled. Victory is mine, whether I can see it or not. I trust when I cannot see. Whatever the price is, YOU have already paid it. Wide-eyed and with heart abandoned, I say YES to You again.

My prayer for you today is that you would let go. Put your hand in His and dance through the fire. He can do this so much better than you. You will be so much stronger on the other side of this because of His strength infusing you. Take the step of faith. You will come out, and you will not even smell like smoke.

> *"Look!" he answered, "I see four men loose, walking in the midst of the fire; and they are not hurt, and the form of the fourth is like the Son of God."* (Dan. 3:25)

> *Now faith is the substance of things hoped for, the evidence of things not seen.* (Heb. 11:1)

Questions:

1. What fire are you facing today? Name the moments you see Jesus in there with you.

2. What Scriptures do you have to stand on and combat the fear, anxiety, or uncertainty that you feel about your current circumstances? List them here and speak them out loud each time those negative emotions arise.

3. Visualize Jesus dancing with you in this season. Just as He parted the Red Sea, He will enable you to triumph over your circumstances. When you see this in your mind, what are the words and thoughts you experience?

Don't Settle—His Best Is on the Way

Do you BELIEVE . . .
God IS Who He says He IS
He WILL do what He said He would do
You ARE who He says YOU ARE.

—Beth Moore

Recently, I was in a position where I had the opportunity to settle for less than His best for me because I was tired of waiting—growing weary in well-doing, beginning to question, is this really what YOU SAID You had for me and mine? I felt like Esau teetering at the edge of destiny with the offer to trade it all in for the bowl of soup that looked really good . . . now. Besides, who am I to think YOU have this GRAND destiny and plans filled with hope and a future for me?

Don't settle at good when GREAT is on the way. Don't stay where you are, just because things have become comfortable. I know it is the easy and convenient choice—today. However, it leads to regret because you chose the less than what was available for you and yours—tomorrow. He said it, and He WILL DO IT. He is not a man that He should lie.

There is a different engine that drives me today than what drove me twelve to thirteen years ago. Then, I was a single mom with a newborn and a toddler, paying off debt, and trying to survive. I worked three jobs still to come up short and depend on God for a miracle every month to make ends meet. And He ALWAYS supplied more than enough. Fuel for survival and charging out of poverty burned at my heels at all times.

Fear of not having enough to provide for my boys dueling with a relentless faith and grit drove me to push hard and long through four promotions. Eventually, that launched me into a position to be extravagantly generous with others in need.

Now I hear Him say, "Don't stop now." I have so much more for you, yours, and those I can touch through you and around you. Now I choose to keep believing that HE IS ABLE to do exceedingly and abundantly above anything I could ever ask for, think of, or even imagine.

How do we move from good to great? How do we step into the more? What does more even look like? Is it just stuff? Is it resources? Is it finances?

More and more, He impresses upon me to seek first the Kingdom of God, and the rest of these things will be added unto me. What is the Kingdom? Love, peace, and joy—this is the Kingdom. Come into His Presence. Seek His face as the priority. Trust Him that out of intimacy with Him, He will give us every desire of our hearts. Then He will use us to be answers and solutions to those around us.

My prayer is that you will press in, go deeper, go longer, go stronger—DON'T STOP. Grit, baby, grit. YOU ARE SO CLOSE to what you have been looking for—and more that you didn't even know was available to you.

> *Being confident of this very thing, that He who has begun a good work in you will complete it until the day of Jesus Christ.* (Phil. 1:6)

> *For I know the thoughts that I think toward you, says the Lord, thoughts of peace and not of evil, to give you a future and a hope. 12 Then you will call upon Me and go and pray to Me, and I will listen to you. 13 And you will seek Me and find Me, when you search for Me with all your heart. 14 I will be found by you, says the Lord, and I will bring you back from your captivity.* (Jer. 29:11–14)

Questions:

1. Where have you had the opportunity to compromise or settle for less than what He has for you? Reflect a moment on this. What steps can you take to stop the compromise?

2. Seek God for what His best is for you in this situation. What has He promised you? What can you do to start reaching for His Promises?

3. What are some ways you can put God and His Kingdom first in your life?

Fill Me Up, God!

> What a beautiful Name it is . . .
> What a wonderful Name it is . . .
> What a powerful Name it is . . .
> Nothing compares to this . . .
> The Name of Jesus.
>
> —Hillsong, "What a Beautiful Name"

A young boy was asking his mom why his father was not a part of their lives, "Doesn't he even care about us? Why doesn't he love us?" Mom was silent for a moment. "He loves you to the best of his ability. He cannot give you what he does not have. We know that God IS love, and wounded people, people without a loving relationship with Him or the inability to receive His love simply cannot give it back to you." Then she smiled to create a lighter moment. "But what you do have is the most amazing mom in the universe, who is head over heels in love with you—and an even MORE AMAZING GOD who promises to be your Father."

Like this young boy, it is so easy to take rejection from people around us, when the reality is they cannot be our source for affirmation or happiness. We go to everyone and everything seeking acceptance and identity. And then we are disappointed and unhappy when they cannot fill our cup.

People get married, enter relationships, have jobs, have children, acquire accomplishments, and/or buy things to feel great about themselves. All these external efforts often leave them disillusioned, unfulfilled, and still hungry for more.

Jesus is the only answer to fill that void in our lives. Your husband is not responsible to fill that void and make you happy. Neither are your children. Multiple accolades and promotions do not create long-term satisfaction. Fabulous vacations, designer handbags, drugs, relationships, the list can go on and on—they do not give you purpose. They do not affirm you. Their presence or lack thereof does not define you.

Every morning, we have to go into His Presence, into His Word to fill up so that we are not expecting others to fill us up. Likewise, sometimes we have to allow Him to heal the broken places so His love and affirmation do not leak back out of us, leaving us needy and desperate.

Likewise, are we filling up until we are overflowing to give out to those around us? Jesus can use us to touch and love a hurting world around us when we are filled up and overflowing from Him as our Source.

I pray today that you go vertical with Him today before going horizontal with the world around you. Trust Him to heal you and make you whole. Trust Him to fill up every empty and dry place in a way that you are completely restored and refreshed.

> *If you abide in Me, and My words abide in you, you will ask what you desire, and it shall be done for you.* (John 15:7)

> *The thief does not come except to steal, and to kill, and to destroy. I have come that they may have life, and that they may have it more abundantly.* (John 10:10)

> *Jesus responded, "What appears humanly impossible is more than possible with God. For God can do what man cannot."* (Luke 18:27)

Questions:

1. Who and what have you been falsely dependent upon for your happiness and affirmation? How can you lay these things and thoughts down to allow Jesus alone to affirm you?

2. Do you find yourself doing things or being someone you are not to receive acceptance from others around you? List some of those things. How can you course correct?

3. Repeat after me. I am accepted and loved by God Almighty. He IS my Source of everything I need. I go to Him to fill my cup, and then I overflow with His glory and goodness onto those around me.

He Knows My Name

You know when I rise and when I fall
When I come or go, You see it all
You hung the stars, and You move the sea
And still You know me
And nothing is hidden from Your sight
Wherever I go, You find me
And You know every detail of my life
'Cause You are God and You don't miss a thing
You know me . . .
You memorize me.

—Bethel Music, "You Know Me"

I love that He knows me inside and out, and He still loves me. My messes, my victories—He knows them all, and He still loves me. There is such peace in knowing He knows the number of hairs on my head, my every thought, the hidden places in my heart, and my dreams and desires.

Jacob wrestled with the angel until God blessed him. He walked away with a limp, and he also walked away with a new name—Israel. He was no longer the deceiver. Now he was Israel, God's chosen people.

As we enter a new season, we often enter in with a new name, a new promise from God to carry us in the good times and bad. This year, He told me that things would happen so fast they would make my head spin. He would pour out blessings like wine coming down the mountains and hills, just because I am His. I heard the scripture about casting my net again, and I would bring in a haul so big I would need help to bring it into the boat. He said, like Abraham, He was doing a new thing. I would leave everything I have known to follow Him.

What He didn't tell me was that I would have to wrestle like Jacob into a place of rest. "What do You want me to do, LORD?" "Be still and know that I AM God." What He left out of our conversation for me to discover on my own was that this year looked more like a valley than a mountaintop—that I would fight pride to arrive at a place of humility, that I would relearn what it meant to serve instead of lead. "What do YOU want me to do LORD?" "Be still and know that I AM God. Watch Me fight this battle on your behalf."

But this feels more like a crushing than a blessing. "My grace is sufficient. The anointing is released in the breaking." This feels more like humiliation than humility. "You are still My child, and that has not changed. Remember who and Whose you are. I will never leave you here."

But . . . "No buts. I AM Who I say I AM. I AM moving mightily on your behalf. You just have to BELIEVE. I change your name, and I call you beautiful."

And this completely wrecks me. To be called beautiful by You, the King of Kings and Lord of LORDS, when I have honestly not been so beautiful in my choices, my responses, my thoughts, my attitude . . . and yet You call me up to that place. I throw myself on Your mercy seat and arrive on the other side of the Refiner's fire. And I say, here I am. LORD. Send me. I say yes. I am past the battle, past the unbelief, anger, and rebellion, past the perceived injustice and the questions with no answers, past the end of me to be embraced by You. Have Your way—it has to be so much better than mine.

I pray you are at the end of you to lay it all down in the beauty of surrender. May you fall into His arms that will hold you so tightly and never let you down. May you look into the eyes of fire of the King of Kings and know He calls you beautiful. May you lay your head on His chest and hear His heartbeat in a rhythm and cadence that calls you in deeper and closer. May you know you are fully loved and accepted as you are. May you answer His call to come up to a new place and to do this new thing He has for you.

> But Lord, your nurturing love is tender and gentle. You are slow to get angry yet so swift to show your faithful love. You are full of abounding grace and truth. (Ps. 86:15)

> Jerusalem will be told: "Don't be afraid. Dear Zion, don't despair. Your God is present among you, a strong Warrior there to save you. Happy to have you back, he'll calm you with his love and delight you with his songs. (Zeph. 3:16–17)

> *But God, being rich in mercy, because of the great love with which He loved us, even when we were dead in our trespasses, made us alive together with Christ— by grace you have been saved.* (Eph. 2:4–5)

Questions:

1. What are you wrestling with during this season? How can you surrender it to Jesus on a daily basis?

2. Spend some time in prayer and surrender, and then ask the Holy Spirit for your new name.

3. Knowing your new name, how will you respond differently in your new nature?

How Bad Do You Want It?

> How bad do you want it?
> I want everything God has for me,
> what does the Word say about it?
> It says resist the devil, and he will flee.
> How bad do you want it?
> I want everything God has for me.
> What does the Word say about it?
> It says greater is He who is in me.
>
> —Karen Wheaton, "Takin' It Back"

The holidays are approaching, and my sons are already relentlessly pursuing their chosen wants for Christmas. We haven't even celebrated Thanksgiving yet. Joshua meets me at the door when I arrive home from work with his various negotiations of how we can obtain this gift together. He wakes up, crawls into my lap, and continues to offer strategy. He could sell last year's presents to put toward the total cost. He could trade in previous years' gifts. He sold his knockoff earbuds to a friend for $20—without the charger because he still needed the charger! Why do I think I am going to receive a call from this child's mother?

My oldest son understands the need for consistency and discipline. I watched him start as an average soccer player, who was slightly insecure when he showed up on the field because he did not work at home. We finally had to have the discussion: If you want to play at this level, it is in you. However, you are going to have to put in the work. Now he shows up to work out and train six days a week, and the difference in his play is from a 1 to a 10. Likewise, his confidence in his abilities is growing, and the outcome is something worthy of praise and thanksgiving to the God Who gave him these gifts and talents.

How often do we want something, and we go to Jesus with our wish list? We offer bribes and negotiations to manipulate circumstances and people to our desired outcome. I think many times, like my plan to buy J his VR headset for Christmas without all of his shenanigans, Jesus plans on giving us the desires of our hearts. When we are walking with Him, He generally put those dreams in our hearts in the first place. He is waiting on something specific in us—or someone else who impacts the execution of this desire.

Sometimes we wait on His timing. Sometimes we obey what He asked us to do. Other times, we must choose to be consistent and disciplined to keep showing up, doing what we know to do. Sometimes we prepare and position ourselves in proximity to the very thing we are asking for from Him. Some things come from fasting and prayer.

How do we know the difference and which route to pursue? First, seek Him for Him alone. Not for a gift. Not for the breakthrough. Not for answers—although He loves to take care of these also. Seek Him, just to be with Him—"Seek ye first the Kingdom of God, and all these things will be added unto you."

Then listen. He often will give you an impression, a Scripture, a Word from someone else to help guide your next footstep. Until that moment, keep consistently showing up in your quiet time. Be disciplined to continue doing the last thing He told you to do with excellence and a great attitude. Praise Him and thank Him for His goodness in your life on a daily basis—it will change your posture and your perspective.

Be willing to lay it down like an Isaac (and don't create an Ishmael by trying to take it into your own hands). Is He the first love of your life? Or is He a means to what you want? It's not that you can't have both. It's that there is an order, and He has to be the priority.

Then be still and know that He IS God, and He IS fighting on your behalf. He will bring every promise over your life to pass. He IS faithful, and He IS always on time. Sometimes the battle is fought on your knees in prayer. Sometimes the answer is found as you praise Him for the answer, confident in Him that it is already on the way. Sometimes it is sowing a seed into the very ground you want to possess. I usually go for all three—knowing He will answer, in spite of my shenanigans.

How bad do you want what He has for you and yours? How relentless are you in pursuing the face of God? How badly do you want to walk in and possess the land He has for you and yours? I pray you would recklessly fall in love with Jesus today. I pray you would have a greater understanding of His all-encompassing love for you. I pray you would set your face like flint to believe in and go after the Promises He has for you and yours. Don't take no for an answer.

Don't stop—even when you're tired and weary. Keep going. Keep pushing. And then rest when it's time to restore and recharge.

Wait on the Lord; Be of good courage, And He shall strengthen your heart; Wait, I say, on the Lord! (Ps. 27:14)

If you abide in Me, and My words abide in you, you will ask what you desire, and it shall be done for you. (John 15:7)

Questions:

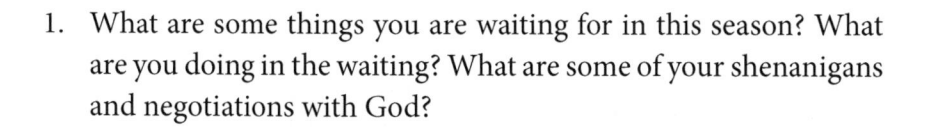

1. What are some things you are waiting for in this season? What are you doing in the waiting? What are some of your shenanigans and negotiations with God?

2. Be still and ask God for direction, clarity, and wisdom. What are you hearing Him say?

3. How bad do you want what He has for you and yours? What are you willing to do and lay down to pursue it with everything that is in you?

Imperfectly Perfect

> You're perfect
> Imperfectly perfect
> You're perfect
> And you know you're worth it
> No one could take your place
> No, you don't have to change
> You're perfect.
>
> —Sophie Michelle, "Imperfectly Perfect"

Some of us go through life like my oldest son; we work hard to try to be the very best at everything we do. We often miss out on things because we didn't do it perfectly the first time, so we don't even attempt it again. We close our minds to the possibilities—and impossibilities we are called to accomplish with God. We are often incredibly hard on ourselves and relentlessly drive ourselves to be and do well, perfect. He may have gotten this from me.

Others face their journey like my youngest. He came home from his first band tryouts:

> J: My teacher says I am the best saxophone player.
> Me: Really? Because you don't read music, and you have never laid eyes, much less hands, on a saxophone before?
> J: Yep.

I heard myself admit recently that I had spent the majority of my adult life trying to be perfect. Perfectly accomplished. Perfectly in shape. Perfectly educated. Perfectly Christian. Perfectly parenting.

(This one breaks the perfectionism in most of us, or we drive everyone insane pretending, demanding.)

One day, I received a revelation of His perfect love for me, just as I am a much-loved child of God. He uses me in spite of me. He favors me and anoints me because of Him in me. He looks at me and sees the blood of Jesus and calls me and blesses me, simply because I am His.

Usually, the right place for excellence is a combination of the two boys' philosophies—somewhere in between these two ditches. Keep the hustle, self-evaluation/awareness, discipline, and planning of one ditch. Keep the childlike faith and confidence of the other. BELIEVE BIG. Partner with God. Be obedient. And watch your life and the lives around you change—through your imperfectly perfect self.

My prayer is that you will surrender every area to Him. He wants to use you, right where you are, just as you are—imperfectly perfect.

> *Most assuredly, I say to you, he who believes in Me, the works that I do he will do also; and greater works than these he will do, because I go to My Father.* (John 14:12)

> *For all the promises of God in Him are Yes, and in Him Amen, to the glory of God through us.* (2 Cor. 1:20)

Questions:

1. In which ditch do you find yourself? How can you move toward the right place in the road of life?

2. What are some areas in your life where you need God's grace to embrace your imperfections? What are some real ways you can do this?

3. How can you allow God to use you right where you are?

In His Presence

I want to sit at Your feet
Drink from the cup in Your hands
Lay back against You and breathe,
Feel Your heartbeat
This love is so deep,
It's more than I can stand
I melt in Your Peace,
It's overwhelming.

—Kari Jobe, "The More I Seek You"

Everything begins and ends in His Presence. I have a saying, "When I don't know what to do, I come back to YOU." Jehoshaphat said it like this: "When I don't know what to do, my eyes are on You." When I hit a roadblock, I go back to the basics of practicing His Presence. When I forget who I am, I crawl up into His lap and say, "Daddy, I don't remember who I am. I don't remember Your Promises and even my purpose anymore."

My boys come to me when they need something—food, school supplies, and new shoes because they have outgrown theirs. They come to me when they want something, whether it's the latest video game, a Frappuccino, or money to spend with friends. They come to me when they have lost something, like their forty-ninth soccer ball, their hoodie, their homework. They come to me when they break something, my windows with said soccer balls, their wall, just because one fell into it (yes, this actually happened). They come to me when they are sick or broken because they know I either have the answer or I am able to get them to someone who does.

While I love and am honored to fulfill all the above, there is no greater moment as a mom than when they come to sit with me—just to be with me. Before I headed out to Brazil for a mission trip, my oldest son lay down beside me on the couch, and we began to reminisce about songs I would sing to him as a little child. One talked about how my hands were bigger than his but one day his little hands would be bigger than mine. We joked, and he said, "I remember thinking, that will NEVER happen!" Then he put his fourteen-year-old hand flush with mine, and his fingertips wrapped over the top of mine.

Today, I pray you would crawl up into the arms of Jesus, just to be with Him. He is more than enough to take care of your needs and wants, brokenness, and wounds. He will help you find what you have lost, even if it's you that has been misplaced. And there is nothing He loves more than to just sit with you and talk about His Promises over your life. He loves to remind you how He has always taken such great care of you, how much He loves you, and share His wisdom with you for the day. Be still and be quiet with Him. He is always speaking to you. Open your heart and open your ears. Let Him fill you up until you are overflowing—the way that only He can.

> *You make known to me the path of life; in Your Presence there is fullness of joy; at Your right hand are pleasures forevermore.* (Ps. 16:11)

> *The mature children of God are those who are moved by the impulses of the Holy Spirit. 15 And you did not receive the "spirit of religious duty," leading you back into the fear of never being good enough. But you have received the "Spirit of full acceptance," enfolding you into the family of God. And you will never feel orphaned, for as he rises up within us, our spirits join him in saying the words of tender affection, "Beloved Father!" 16 For the Holy Spirit makes God's fatherhood real to us as he whispers into our innermost being, "You are God's beloved child!"* (Rom. 8:14–16)

Questions:

1. How are you currently practicing the Presence of God in your daily life? How can you increase this practice to experience more of God's Presence?

2. Are you willing and able to crawl into His lap without an agenda and be still in His Presence? Are you listening to what He is saying?

3. Take five minutes of just being still with Him. Write down what you hear and see. Let His love wash over you and refresh you.

Jesus, Have Your Way

> Lord, I give You my heart
> I give You my soul
> I live for YOU alone
> Every breath that I take
> Every moment I'm awake
> LORD, have Your way in me.
>
> —Hillsong Worship, "I Give You My Heart"

My oldest son often asks me what he should eat and how he should work out to gain weight (something that doesn't even resonate with me). Because of my background in both fitness and nutrition, I start to share ideas. He immediately starts shaking his head and says, "Nah, I'm good." I finally asked him, "Why do you ask me when you are just saying no? You waste my time and energy, and your mind is already predetermined not to go that direction."

Immediately, I heard His whisper in my heart. *Why do My people ask Me and then ignore or compromise My answer?* "Use me, Lord. I say YES!" And then at the first sign of discomfort or inconvenience: "Oh, Lord, get me out of this situation" or "Don't use me that way."

I have worked out and eaten relatively healthy for the majority of my life. I worked out up until the day I gave birth to my children, and I was working out again less than two weeks later; one was two days later—I DO NOT recommend this. There is a fine line between perseverance and stupidity, and I found myself on the other side with this one.

Yet when people around me want to lose weight and get in shape, they do not receive my answers. They would rather try fad diets and a quick fix versus move more and eat less. Likewise, we often crave faith to move mountains, but we limit God and what He will do in our lives because we are not willing to sacrifice or work out our faith muscles to do and be what He is asking us to do and be.

I remember the story of the little girl with the fake strand of pearls. Every night, her daddy would ask her for her pearls. She would tell him no time and time again because the dime-store necklace was her special treasure. She would offer everything else she had, but not these pearls. Finally, she gave in with tears in her eyes to hand him the pearls of no real value. In return, he placed in her hands a beautiful strand of authentic, rare, and valuable pearls.

Sometimes we have to let go of what we treasure—our independence, our stuff, our hidden places, our comfort. We let go to give Him permission to fill our hands with something even better.

I pray that today we would ask Him where we can partner with Him to touch the world around us. I pray we would let down the barriers of every hidden place to allow Him to do a deep surgery. I pray we would let go of our comfort and security to step into that BIG place He has called us. I pray that we would allow Him to build our faith muscles to the place that we move mountains and slay giants. Today, I pray that He would completely have His way in us.

> *Now it shall come to pass, if you diligently obey the voice of the* Lord *your God, to observe carefully all His commandments which I command you today, that the* Lord *your God will set you high above all nations of the earth.[2] And all these blessings shall come upon you and overtake you, because you obey the voice of the* Lord *your God:*
> *[3]Blessed shall you be in the city and blessed shall you be in the country.*
> *[4]Blessed shall be the fruit of your body, the produce of your ground and the increase of your herds, the increase of your cattle and the offspring of your flocks.*
> *[5]Blessed shall be your basket and your kneading bowl.*
> *[6]Blessed shall you be when you come in and blessed shall you be when you go out.* (Deut. 28:1–6)

Questions:

1. What are the questions you have recently asked the LORD? Has He ever responded to you with answers you did not receive? Has He asked you to do some things that you don't want to do?

2. What is He asking you to do in this season? What are the action steps you can take to be obedient?

3. How are you limiting God in your life? How can you remove those limitations to walk more fully in ALL HE HAS FOR YOU!

Legacy

> When You don't move the mountains, I'm needing You to move
> When You don't part the waters, I wish I could walk through
> When You don't give the answers, as I cry out to YOU,
> I will trust, I will trust, I will trust in You.
>
> —Lauren Daigle, "Trust in You"

There came a transition in my career where leadership was no longer about me and my climb up the corporate ladder, the place where high performance and achievement were no longer the mission and reward. True leadership begins when the purpose becomes about seeing your people succeed and become their best versions of themselves versus what they can do for you.

As I walk on this journey with Jesus, I realize there is always this juxtaposition of concepts that are counterintuitive to our natural instincts. We plant seeds of giving, and we reap a harvest of financial freedom. We serve, and we walk in promotion and leadership. We forgive those who do us wrong, and we walk in love, joy, and peace. We choose praise, worship, and thanksgiving to wage war. We trust a God we cannot see, and yet we see and hear Him all around us.

One of my favorites is the reality that He is so wildly in love with us. He constantly blesses us and surrounds us with favor like a shield. He is for us, who can be against us? All things are truly possible with and in Him. He cares about everything that pertains to us. He gives us answers to have strong marriages, raise Godly children, financial success and stability and how to win at life.

Yet it's not all about us. We are part of a much bigger puzzle. Our piece is significant. More importantly, our piece impacts the puzzles around us.

I remember transitioning out of poverty into a place of above-average means. I hear in my heart, *There is so much more. Don't stop here. What I have is more than you ever thought possible. Don't settle for above average, when you have been called to be extraordinary.* Likewise, I would do a heart check, what is more? Why do you want the more? What would you do, and who would you be if you had whatever more is?

Finally, the right answer dropped into my spirit. I want everything God has for me and mine. Everything He has spoken over us for our Promised Land, that is what I want—nothing more, and nothing less. I don't want the more-for stuff. I want more to finance more mission trips to take His Word and His love to the people around the world who are crying out to be rescued. I want to help the family down the street who lost their jobs. I want to help the single mom who cannot pay her bills or spend time with her children because of her three jobs. I want to help fund the ministry that is pulling prostitutes off the streets. I want more to help more and do more and be more—MORE LIKE JESUS.

When I look into the brown eyes of my boys, I want to be and do all I have been called to be and do. When I sit across from young leaders I mentor or from my pastors, I don't want to stop until I have laid my life down for the call that is awakened in me. When I hold my eighteen-month-old niece, hug my baby sister, or kiss my mom's cheeks, I want to leave a legacy behind that draws them all into a more intimate relationship with Christ. When my time here is over, I want my oversized gas tank to be on E because I have poured out until there is nothing left—and You to say to me, "Well done, My good and faithful servant . . . Well done, beloved."

I pray today that you would get up and walk this thing called life out to its fullest. May you reach your fullest potential. May you fill up and pour out over and over and over again. May you not stop. May you not become complacent in okay or above average. May you not quit because you think it's too hard. Do it for Him. Do it for yourself. Do it for your children. Do it for all those around you. Do it because it's like a fire shut up in your bones that you absolutely cannot contain.

Keep pushing. The mountains will move. The water will part. The answer is here—and His Name is Jesus.

> *And let us not grow weary while doing good, for in due season we shall reap if we do not lose heart.* (Gal. 6:9)

> *A good man leaves an inheritance to his children's children, But the wealth of the sinner is stored up for the righteous.* (Prov. 13:22)

> *For assuredly, I say to you, if you have faith as a mustard seed, you will say to this mountain, 'Move from here to there,' and it will move; and nothing will be impossible for you.* (Matt. 17:20)

Questions:

1. As a leader in your spheres of influence (could be at home, work, church, or community), how are you investing in and growing those around you?

2. What is the legacy you want to leave behind? What are some ways you can start to do this? Remember, the small and consistent things do add up more quickly than you realize.

3. What are areas in your life that He has delivered, healed, and restored you? How can you help others facing these same situations?

Lies and Timelines

You say I am loved when I can't feel a thing
You say I am strong when I think I am weak
And you say I am held when I am falling short
And when I don't believe, You say I am Yours
And I believe, Oh I believe,
What YOU say of me.

—Lauren Daigle, "You Say"

I was driving on some country roads to return a truck I had borrowed during a move in a time when cell phones were the large bag phones and there were few cell towers out in the country. The truck broke down, it's late at night, and I could not see a house anywhere near me.

I did what I always do in a crisis. I began to pray. I started walking in a direction, thinking I will eventually run into a house with people. After about thirty minutes of walking, I saw a house. I went to knock on the door, and a dog came running at me. Having been bit by a dog as a child, I already had some irrational fears about dogs charging at me. I froze and began to pray in the Spirit and proclaim the name of Jesus, not because I am super spiritual, but because it was the only coherent thing I could do.

The dog barked in circles all around me, but never touched me. The door finally opened, and the wide-eyed lady took her dog in hand. She said, "I can't believe he didn't just rip you to shreds." Silently, I thought, *Yeah, same.*

Once I was back on my way, I began to process the situation, and the Holy Spirit whispered to me, "That dog is like the enemy. All he can do is bark at you. He only has the power you give him. As long as you are cloaked in My Presence, he cannot harm you, only speak lies. Ultimately, you have to choose to agree with his lies, and then they lead to fear, discouragement, despair, and the list of every negative emotion."

Over the years, I hear this lesson again to uncover the lies I am choosing to believe, lies that are holding me back from the goodness God has for my life. Lies that hold me back from what He wants to pour through me to touch someone else. I am not smart enough, pretty enough, rich enough, skinny enough, Christian enough, all the not-enough statements we all battle or accept in our minds. We will never be enough. He uses us in that not-enough place, and He is our strength where we are weak.

Recent lies I have uncovered are timelines I have set up in my head. Some people compare themselves to others. I compare myself to these timelines I have established in my mind of who I should be and where I should be at this point in my life.

I began to become discouraged and anxious. I am behind on my college funds for the boys. I am behind on my long-term financial plan. I am behind on being married and building a life with a spouse. The boys are about to graduate, so they will never experience having a father in the house to look up to as a male role model. I am not the CEO I thought I would be by now. I have not accomplished everything I set out to accomplish.

Finally, the Lord stopped me. He said, "Who told you that you were behind? My one touch suddenly can change everything in a moment. What IF you are right on time? What if you are right where I want you to be, completely dependent on Me? Have I ever failed you? Have I ever let you down? Does My arm wax short? Am I an abusive Father that I would give you a taste of your dreams and desires and then take them all away?"

I pray today you would see and know that you are more than enough in Him. I pray you would rest in His timeline over your life and know that He is the Author and Finisher of your faith. He WILL complete the good work He has begun in you.

And the LORD will make you the head and not the tail; you shall be above only and not beneath, if you heed the commandments of the LORD *your God, which I command you today, and are careful to observe them.* (Deut. 28:13)

Yet in all these things we are more than conquerors through Him Who loved us. (Rom. 8:37)

The steps of a good man are ordered by the LORD, and He delights in his way. (Ps. 37:23)

Questions:

1. What lies have you been listening to from the enemy? Ask God to reveal these to you. Write them down and replace them with God's Promises. Each time that lie rises up, cast it down with God's Word.

2. What are the timelines in your head? Where do you feel behind, not enough, or anxious? Hand those timelines to Him. He is ALWAYS right on time.

3. What are your "not-enough" statements that play like a broken record in your mind? List them out. Then ask God to breathe on each one to show you what He thinks about you in each of these areas. You ARE MORE THAN ENOUGH in HIM.

Live in the Present—Enjoy the Process

Live in the present, not the future, and certainly not the past. Never spend all the time regretting events that have already passed or worrying about what may happen. Accept that you can't change the past, but that you have a large amount of control over what you do in the present, which will influence your future.

—Dr. Anil Kinha

I had an MBA assignment to ask those closest to me about my blind spots and how to improve to become a better leader. One of my dearest and closest colleagues said something that redefined the way I looked at how I handled business, personal, and anything related to people and time.

She said, "You have a gift that draws people to you. They want to touch and share the peace, joy, love, and wisdom that you carry. You are always positive, encouraging, and help us see the very best in ourselves and others." I sensed a *but*—"Your world has become so incredibly busy, that when you are here, you are not really here."

I wanted to explain the demands of this new senior-level position. I wanted to tell her about my phone days being scheduled in fifteen-minute increments, flying away from my home and family every week of my life, people following me to the bathroom during meetings for just five minutes of my time. And yet, I knew what she said was true, and none of those things mattered. I saw it in the longing of my children's faces when the phone would ring one more time on Saturday night at nine.

Be present. Whatever you are doing in that moment, engage and do it well. There are days when I would hang up all this executive leadership stuff and just be a child of God and a mom to my sweet boys, young men now. Days when I would tuck away my passport for another season to just be present. Now, I know some of you stay-at-home moms would love to have a day at the office to regain your sanity and put on lipstick and high heels—maybe.

Whatever season and moment we find ourselves in, let's do it well. Let's be thankful, focus on what is positive, learn what we need to learn here, and influence and love the one that is placed in front of us. The way we do this place determines the amount of time we spend here and the doors that open and close around us. The way we exit this place is the way we enter the next.

God is more interested in relationship and process versus just moving you from point A to point B. Everything is a journey and a process. Embrace where you are on the way to where you are going. God always meets you where you are, and He will never leave you there. While I am here, I will lead well. I will serve well, and I will love well with a grateful heart. I will be fully present when I am at work. I will be fully present when I am home. I will create and give both quality and quantity deposits into my worlds. Likewise, I will keep Jesus my number one priority in the midst of all this to provide me with wisdom and strategy to balance and do it with excellence.

Likewise, I will dream BIG and look for those divine footsteps, doors, and connections that He has for us. I will prepare by sitting in His Presence and being obedient when He says go and when He says be still.

As I sit on the twelfth birthday of my baby, I remember holding him while singing, "If I could just hold you . . . this moment in time . . . make every moment count." It's these moments that build the realities of your tomorrow. One moment in the Presence of God forever changed the life of the woman with the issue of blood. One moment, one touch—it's all you need.

Be still and know that I AM God. (Ps. 46:10)

And since we are his true children, we qualify to share all his treasures, for indeed, we are heirs of God himself. And since we are joined to Christ, we also inherit all that He is and all that He has. We will experience being co-glorified with Him provided that we accept His sufferings as our own. (Rom. 8:17)

Questions:

1. Ask God to reveal areas of your life where you are not present. Write them down, along with ideas of how to be more present. Have a friend be your accountability partner in these areas.

2. Where are some places you can make better quality and quantity time and resource deposits? What would this look like in a practical manner?

3. What season are you in today? How can you do this season with excellence?

Look Like Jesus—In Your Unique Expression

> Take me, Mold me
> Use me, Fill me
> I give my life to the Potter's hands
> Hold me, Guide me
> Lead me, Walk beside me.
>
> —Darlene Zschech, "The Potter's Hand"

My son often tells me that I may have learned to control my mouth, but my face still tells exactly what I am thinking—and it may or may not look like Jesus. It's a test I have taken on more than one occasion, and I do not always pass.

I was sitting on a couch in the gym writing a devotion while he was working out. For the record, I had worked out that morning. I was also ministering to someone via text and completing the lesson I had started. The hall monitor of the gym approached me, and she said she needed to clean the couch I was sitting on—and I am positive I flunked the test of drawing her unto Christ by allowing His goodness to flow out of me and touch her (insert rolling-eyes emoji here).

My immediate thought was, *There are 4,000 pieces of equipment in this gym, and you need to wipe down the one couch I am sitting on . . . for real?* I heard, "Look like Jesus. You are a Bible study teacher." Sigh. I did the right thing, reeled it in, and went to my car to wait on my son.

I know the Word says I am fearfully and wonderfully made. I often ask the LORD why He naturally made me so fiery and passionate because it takes a whole lot of Jesus (and time outs) to help me behave myself. There are times I throw a grenade when I am pretty sure. He said, "Be still and know that I AM God . . . let Me fight this battle for you." Right. Please make all things work together for my good . . . and theirs too.

I bring new levels of meaning to "He takes the foolish things of this world and makes them wise" because truly if He can use me the way He does, He can use ANYONE. When I submit (I sometimes choke on this word . . . just being real), He does INCREDIBLE and life-changing things in me and for others. Without Him, I become a complete idiot in about three seconds flat.

He specifically made me to touch a group of people and change things in history in a way that no one else can. I carry a spiritual DNA of gifts and talents to believe for and execute His assignment to make a difference in my spheres of influence in a way that only I can. Someone's breakthrough is waiting on my obedience and my willingness to overcome my will, fears, and obstacles around me.

Every famous person in the Bible had to overcome and win in the wilderness season to do the great things He had called them to do. Likewise, He is no respecter of persons, and what He did for them and me, He wants to do in you also.

My prayer for you today is that you say yes, that you would embrace everything about you and submit it to Him. He will refine you and use you in ways you never thought possible. Be willing. Be obedient. Be okay with being uncomfortable. Be okay with walking blindly by faith, knowing that HE IS ABLE. He IS MORE THAN ENOUGH.

> *Never doubt God's mighty power to work in you and accomplish all this. He will achieve infinitely more than your greatest request, your most unbelievable dream, and exceed your wildest imagination! He will outdo them all, for his miraculous power constantly energizes you.* (Eph. 3:20)

> *Eye has not seen, nor ear heard, nor have entered the heart of man the things which God has prepared for those who love Him.* (1 Cor. 2:9)

Questions:

1. Do you need some more self-control in your thoughts, words, actions, and facial expressions? What are some examples of where you have passed the test? Others where you may have the opportunity to retake it?

2. What are some action steps you can take to have a better response next time or at least reel it in during the process?

3. What are your least favorite things about your personality? How can you submit these areas to God and allow Him to use you?

Love the One in Front of You

> Way Maker, Miracle Worker
> Promise Keeper, Light in the Darkness,
> My God, that is Who You ARE . . .
> Even when I don't see it, You're working
> Even when I don't feel it, You're working
> You never stop, You never stop working.
>
> —Sinach, "Way Maker"

I was visiting one of our campuses for a Sunday service, and I had just asked the LORD to use me to represent Him in this place: "Show me how to love the one You place in front of me." Pastor Crystal Sparks was preaching about the parables of the woman going after the one lost coin, the shepherd going after the one lost sheep, and the father going after the one lost prodigal son. She compared that to Jesus always going after the one lost child.

All day, every day, we have the opportunity to be the hands, feet, mouth, and heartbeat of Jesus. If we are in tune with His Presence and willing to be obedient, He will make multiple divine touch points that will make a difference. In the span of one hour, I had the opportunity to be reminded of the impact my obedience had on someone twelve years ago by being obedient with a gift. This woman is a beautiful wife, mother, and excelling in everything she puts her hand to today. What an honor to know that a simple act of obedience and love was a part of leading her to this place.

I was able to hug several of the children, now teenagers, that used to hang around with my boys when we lived in the area. I always pray my home is a place that shares the love and peace of Jesus to every person who walks through our doors. Likewise, the stories of each of these children have had a profound impact on my life and the lives of my boys.

I was able to use pieces of my testimony to speak into a young man's life, who was floundering in his journey—discouraged and deflated in this place. I took the time to take him home, and he made the simple comment of how thankful he was for someone to speak hope and encouragement in a world that did not make this available to him.

I was able to wrap my arms around one of our leaders and tell her she is not alone in this place. God has such incredible plans for her life, and a company of people is coming around her to support her and be a safe and soft place for her. I didn't know her story. I felt odd saying those words, and yet I know they were from the heart of God.

None of these things cost me anything. They represented a little time and a little effort, but nothing replaces the reward of seeing lightbulbs go on, smiles and eyes lighting up the room, and to know that God could trust a woman like me (sometimes a complete hot mess) to be faithful in the little things He asked me to do.

I don't always have the privilege of seeing the outcome. Sometimes it's me that needs the word of encouragement, the hug that says I am not alone, or the confirmation that my obedience made a difference. I also think of all the missed opportunities when I am moving too fast, inwardly focused, or just at a place that I am not as quick to obey. There is no condemnation in Christ, but my heart's cry is to grow in looking and acting more like Him.

Today, I pray you are tuned in and listening to the heart of the Father. I pray you are obedient to the sound of His voice to love the people He places in your path. Some people that look like they have it all together need a touch from Him the most, so don't judge by appearances. Don't shy away from the ones that are forgotten or neglected. Don't pick and choose which opportunities you take. Choose the ones He has already chosen for you.

The one who manages the little he has been given with faithfulness and integrity will be promoted and trusted with greater responsibilities. (Luke 16:10)

So I give you now a new commandment: Love each other just as much as I have loved you. 35 For when you demonstrate the same love I have for you by loving one another, everyone will know that you're my true followers. (John 13:34–35)

Since we are approaching the end of all things, be intentional, purposeful, and self-controlled so that you can be given to prayer. 8 Above all, constantly echo God's intense love for one another, for love will be a canopy over a multitude of sins. (1 Pet. 4:7–8)

Questions:

1. Who is the one in front of you that Jesus is asking you to love? How can you love this person with words and actions?

2. What simple act of obedience and love can you participate in today?

3. Where and with whom can you share pieces of your testimony or some encouragement today? Make a commitment to be intentional about this over the course of the next seven days.

More than Enough—In Him

> I'm not enough unless You come
> Will You meet me here again
> 'Cause all I want is all You are
> Will You meet me here again?
>
> —Elevation Worship, "Here Again"

Every time I stand up to speak on the mission field, sit down to write, minister, or coach one-on-one, or even step into some of the work positions God has placed me, inadequacy and insecurity hit me in waves that want to overwhelm me and take my feet out from under me.

I remember my first position in health care in my early thirties. I thought daily, *If they ever figure out I have no idea what I am doing, they are going to fire me.* Holy Spirit would whisper in my heart, "No man can take away what I have given you. You can give it away with your mouth and words or by simply giving up. But no one can take it away from you. You can rest in that Truth."

Each time He called me to the mission field or into another promotion at work, I would argue with Him, "But I have nothing to say, nothing to give." And He would remind me that He is more than enough in me. He would whisper to me, "Give me what you have, and like the little boy with the two fish and five loaves of bread, I will take it, multiply it, and feed the masses with it."

God will never call you to be easy and comfortable. If your dreams don't scare you, then you are dreaming alone versus dreaming with God. He will always call you to a place where you have to depend on

Him, be in relationship and partnership with Him, and implicitly trust in Him to see those Promises come to pass.

His Word says He IS able to do exceedingly and abundantly above anything you could ever ask for, think of, or even imagine. He says that truly no eye can see, no ear can hear, and no mind can conceive the good things He has for you. That crazy, wild dream on the inside of you, the one that has you questioning your sanity, the one where the enemy asks you, "Who do you think you are?" You are not enough, and you will never be worthy to carry it but God. When you abide in Him, He says you are the righteousness of God in Christ Jesus. His Word says He orders your every footstep. Abide. Trust. Obey. Believe He will do it—in you, with you, through you, and for you.

I pray today that you would see yourself wrapped in His love and His Presence. I pray you would see those mountains and barriers melting like wax in His powerful Presence. I pray you would begin to dream again and believe for the great and mighty plans He has for you and yours.

> *4 Abide in Me, and I in you. As the branch cannot bear fruit of itself, unless it abides in the vine, neither can you, unless you abide in Me. 5 "I am the vine, you are the branches. He who abides in Me, and I in him, bears much fruit; for without Me you can do nothing. 6 If anyone does not abide in Me, he is cast out as a branch and is withered; and they gather them and throw them into the fire, and they are burned. 7 If you abide in Me, and My words abide in you, you will ask what you desire, and it shall be done for you. 8 By this My Father is glorified, that you bear much fruit; so you will be My disciples. (John 15:4–8)*

Questions:

1. What insecurities in what places do you fight?

2. What is He asking you to give Him so that He can multiply it and use it for His glory?

3. What is the crazy, wild dream you have on the inside of you? How can you trust God with your dreams? What are you doing to release that dream into a reality?

On My Knees in the Midst of the Storm

> Sometimes it's hard to breathe
> All these thoughts they shout at me
> Try to bring me to my knees
> And it's overwhelming
> Darkness echoes all around
> Feels like everything is crashing down
> Still I know where my hope is found
> And it's only You...
> Through all of this chaos
> You are writing a symphony.
>
> —Switch, "Symphony"

Some of you may be more mature than me, and you are capable of sleeping in the middle of the storm. I have not arrived at that place to date. However, I do know how to get on my knees, arms lifted to Heaven, and simply say, "I don't know what to do, but my eyes are on YOU, JESUS. You have never let me down, and YOU ARE not starting now. You love me, and YOU ARE for me. You ARE working all things together for my good."

There are times in life where fear tries to strangle us. When our jobs and only means of support for our families are on the line, when we hear an intimidating diagnosis in our health, when someone we love is at risk, these moments when it seems hopeless, a dead end, nowhere to turn. In these moments, all the lies and what-ifs start barraging our minds. What if I cannot provide for my children? What if we have to move somewhere else to find work? What if our health declines? What if they don't make it? What if...

And I hear the Holy Spirit say, "Breathe. I have you in the palms of My Almighty hands. Be still. Know that I AM God. I AM already working everything together for your good. You can trust Me. You can count on me. Don't look with your natural eyes. Look at My Word and what it says about you and your situation."

You are the head and not the tail. Above and not beneath. More than a conqueror in Christ Jesus. You are blessed in the city, blessed in the field, blessed coming in and going out. This battle belongs to the LORD. The children of God will never be begging for bread. He takes care of the birds of the air and the lilies of the field, how much more will He take care of you, his blessed children?

He IS the Alpha and Omega, Beginning and the End. He owns the cattle on a thousand hills. The enemy may have come to steal, kill, and destroy. But He came that we could have life abundantly. GREATER is He that is in me than he that is in this world. He IS the God of the Impossible. King of Kings. LORD of LORDS. He IS my Daddy, and He takes such GREAT CARE of me.

And I breathe in and out until I can rest . . . until there is nothing left to do, but trust a God Who IS SO MUCH BIGGER and GREATER than me or my circumstances.

Peter once said, "Who else would we follow?" It was like YOU ARE the only choice. I can worry and fret in this moment. I can buy into all the what-ifs. Or I can say, I trust YOU. Above all else, I trust YOU. You Are the One Who has always loved me. You have always taken care of me and mine—miraculously delivered me time and time and time and time again.

Part the Red Sea. Move the mountain. Deliver me from the hands of my enemies. Wrap me and mine in a hedge of protection beneath Your wings—in the secret place. There is no place I would rather be than here—on my knees, trusting YOU to do it again, BETTER than I could ever ask for, think of, or even imagine. Selah.

> *Fear not, for I am with you; Be not dismayed, for I am your God. I will strengthen you, Yes, I will help you, I will uphold you with My righteous right hand. 11 Behold, all those who*

were incensed against you shall be ashamed and disgraced; They shall be as nothing, And those who strive with you shall perish. 12 You shall seek them and not find them—Those who contended with you. Those who war against you shall be as nothing, As a nonexistent thing. 13 For I, the Lord your God, will hold your right hand, saying to you, "Fear not, I will help you." (Isa. 41:10–13)

Questions:

1. What storms are you currently facing? What are some examples of how Jesus has rescued you when you were facing a storm before? Does that help you to believe He WILL do it again?

2. What are some places that what-ifs and lies are overwhelming you? How can you rewrite the script and trust Jesus?

3. Take and write down some of the Promises from above that apply to the current storm in your circumstances. When fear and anxiety raise their heads, declare these Promises out loud until you wrestle your way back to peace.

Our Response in the Waiting

> Slow down, take time
> Breathe in He said
> He'd reveal what's to come
> The thoughts in His mind
> Always higher than mine . . .
> Take courage my heart
> Stay steadfast my soul
> He's in the waiting
> Hold onto your hope
> As your triumph unfolds
> He's never failing.
>
> —Bethel, "Take Courage"

Waiting—this is probably one of my least favorite words. I am the person that gives Christmas presents in November because I don't want to wait until Christmas Day. We celebrate Christmas for the entire month of December because I love to find creative ways to make sure we remember the reason for the season, and I love to see my boys' and friends' faces light up when they receive a gift at any point during the month.

I prefer the Express Lane because I shave ten to fifteen minutes of time off my drive. I order my Starbucks via app when I leave the gym because it's ready when I drive into the parking lot. I entertained myself on my phone at red lights—until I realized how valuable praying in these moments would be for me and my relationship with Jesus. I shop on Amazon, have auto ship on most things, and do as much online as possible. I arrive early to any work function with specific items to complete lined out so I can continue being productive until the meeting starts. I show up as late as possible without being rude to social functions, well, because these aren't my favorite, because you wait around and you're not very productive, and God's still working on me here.

The average person spends six months waiting in line and forty-three days on hold for automated systems. We wait in doctors' offices, and we wait in restaurants. We wait for the Defensive Driving class to be over for those of us who couldn't wait in traffic and paid the price for our impatience. We wait.

With so much waiting, you would think we would be professional waiters when it comes to God's promises over our lives, and yet . . . most of us don't do this well. King David waited thirty years before becoming king after he was anointed to lead Israel. During that thirty years, he battled for his life, ran, and hid in caves and was rejected over and over again.

And yet when I have to wait twelve years for some unanswered promises, I find myself growing weary in well-doing. I find myself doubting that I heard God right the first time, doubting that He will do this in my life, doubting that He has these plans and purposes over my life. As long as I stay in this mentality, I will stay in the waiting. My attitude, ability to rest with calm expectation, obedience, willingness to continue to believe beyond what my eyes can see, and perseverance determines much of the waiting period. Sometimes God is waiting for someone else in each of these areas. Sometimes it's more about the process of leaning into relationship with Him. Sometimes He's growing your character and your capacity to be able to carry this next assignment with excellence and in a way that brings glory to Him.

In this season of waiting FOREVER and ETERNITY (yes, I can still act five years old), I am learning to seek Him first, and He will add these things to me. I continue to declare His Promises—He will make this happen so fast it will make my head spin. I will cast this net again and trust Him to help me bring in a haul so big. I will call my future into my present. I will believe that He has incredible plans for our lives. I will trust that He will give me the desires of my heart.

After seeking Him, I will serve Him and the people He has placed around me. I will sow seeds of pouring into those around me to help them arrive at the other side of their waiting. I will celebrate their wins, even when it looks like the wins I want for my life. I will keep pointing them back to Jesus. I will love them right where they are to help them open their hearts to hear Him to take them where they want to be. I will keep doing the things He has asked me to do until He releases the next assignment in me and through me.

My prayer today is that you turn to Him in the waiting. Open your heart again to receive all that He has for you—even if it takes some time. Enjoy the process and the journey. Receive a revelation of how much He loves you. Know that He IS for you, who can be against you? Know He IS already working on your behalf, and the answer is on its way. Keep praising Him. Keep thanking Him. Keep knowing that He IS able and willing, and your breakthrough is within reach.

> *I wait for the LORD, my soul waits, and in His Word I hope, my soul waits.* (Ps. 130:5–6)

> I would have lost heart, unless I had believed that I would see the goodness of the LORD in the land of the living. ¹⁴ Wait on the LORD; be of good courage, and He shall strengthen your heart; wait, I say, on the LORD! (Ps. 27:13–14)

> Trust in the Lord completely, and do not rely on your own opinions. With all your heart rely on him to guide you, and he will lead you in every decision you make. ⁶ Become intimate with him in whatever you do, and he will lead you wherever you go. *Trust in the LORD with all your heart, and do not lean on your own understanding. In all your ways acknowledge Him, and He will make straight your paths.* (Prov. 3:5–6)

Questions:

1. Where do you see yourself being impatient and not waiting well?

2. What are some Godly practices you can implement during the waiting process?

3. List God's Promises over your life and the places you doubt you heard Him. Begin to believe again, and trust that He is faithful to fulfill every Promise.

Out of These Ashes—Hope Will Arise

> I raise a hallelujah, in the presence of my enemies . . .
> Louder than my unbelief . . .
> My weapon is a melody . . .
> Heaven comes to fight for me . . .
> I'm gonna sing in the middle of the storm.
>
> —Bethel, "Raise a Hallelujah"

This past season has been one of my more difficult seasons. I have experienced unanswered prayers that have taken longer than I ever thought they would and answered prayers that looked different than I thought.

In the disappointment, in the battle, weary from well-doing without the anticipated reward or outcome, I caught myself backing away, backing away from the Promises, backing away from the call, backing away from the pain associated with hope deferred.

In the middle of all this, I continued with the basics of what I knew was right in spite of the fact that I didn't want to participate. I still showed up consistently in my quiet time. I still went to church and engaged. I still poured out to people, even when I really didn't feel like it. I still chose to find gratitude and encouragement for others, celebrations for their wins, even when it felt like pieces of me were lying down and dying on the inside.

A sweet friend asked me if I was happy. I started to answer with the Christian answer—I choose to be happy. Happiness is a choice . . . and it is. I thought about this beautiful, strong, and amazing woman listening to my response. She has nine children of her own and then adopted over ten additional children. She recently lost her husband

and lost a son much too soon. She didn't need the typical Christian answer. She needed my authenticity and raw transparency.

I described the loneliness, the frustration, the disappointment, and yes, even anger—more with the situation, but at times honestly aiming it at God because He knew my heart. I would tell Him, "I know YOU could remedy these situations, and yet for some reason, You choose to leave me here."

I went on to tell her that my circumstances had not really changed, but God is changing me in the circumstances. Hope is rising out of these ashes, and He IS breathing His breath of life on the dry bones of my dreams. He is restoring purpose and vision, as I completely lay down my will into His Hands in complete surrender.

Philippians is often considered the happy book of the Bible, and yet Paul wrote these words from a jail cell after being brutally beaten for his obedience. As Paul and Silas worshipped in their darkest hour, their chains fell off, and the prison doors flew open. Not only were they set free, but everyone around them was also set free because they chose to offer the sacrifice of praise and worship. They chose to BELIEVE what they could not see.

On the threshing floor and the mercy seat, I said, "I choose to believe that YOU ARE for me, who can be against me? I choose to sit under the shadow of Your Almighty wings and trust that YOU ARE a good God, who is wildly in love with me. I choose to BELIEVE, if Your answer is not now, then Your yes will be so much GRANDER than I could ever imagine."

I pray today that you come to the end of yourself and fall into the arms of Jesus. It's a free fall, and it's really scary and uncomfortable. Yet I know He IS faithful—for both of us. I will cast the net again with hope and faith and BELIEVE that I will bring in a haul so big that I will need help to contain it.

> *But seek first the Kingdom of God and His Righteousness, and all these things shall be added to you.* (Matt. 6:33)

Yes, indeed, it won't be long now . . . Things are going to happen so fast your head will swim, one thing fast on the heels of the other. You won't be able to keep up. Everything will be happening at once—and everywhere you look, blessings! Blessings like wine pouring off the mountains and hills. (Amos 9:13–15)

Questions:

1. What unanswered prayers are you waiting on to hear and see from God? List them here, and begin to pray again like you expect Him to answer you.

2. What prayers look different than you thought? List them here. Be thankful. See His fingerprints and footsteps in your life.

3. What are some ways and words you can praise Him for the place you are now while you are on the way to where He is taking you?

Seeing Him in Everyday Life

> Amazing grace, how sweet the sound
> That saved a wretch like me
> I once was lost, but now I am found
> I was blind, but now I see.
>
> —John Newton, "Amazing Grace"

I have been blessed to travel to some of the most amazing places in the world—Italy (my favorite), Paris, Germany, Vietnam, Brazil, Aruba, Dominican Republic, Hawaii, Jamaica, Barbados, Anguilla, Costa Rica, Cabo, just to name my top picks.

Yet I sit here in my living room with the lights low, as we are wrapping up the Thanksgiving holiday, and I would say today has been the most perfect day. I sat in my pajamas this morning with a cup of coffee over an extended quiet time. This is a rare jewel because I usually have a 7:00 AM workout with one of my dearest friends—for accountability and fellowship. Also, I do not typically have sleep-in days (6:00 AM is sleeping in for my world).

Then I had church with my sweet boys, a.k.a. young men, younger sister and her family, and one of my other dearest friends. We had a great message about how God is with us during the storms—resting and letting go of control. (Three people turned and emphasized this point with me. WHHAATT! Clearly, they do not see my growth.) I had some great connections with some great friends today and lunch with Mrs. Miriam and the boys.

I still did my beast-mode leg workout with my baby sister and oldest son—six sets of eight exercises back to back. Even with something random in my eye that would not go away the entire time

I worked out . . . grrrrrr. I won't mention how ridiculous I looked with no makeup on one eye. No, I do not typically put on makeup for the gym, but it was left over from church.

I did slightly drool over pictures of the Amalfi Coast sent by a great friend, who is currently experiencing my dream vacation, Venice (he even had the gondola ride), Florence, Tuscany, Capri, and the Amalfi Coast.

Now I am back in clean said pajamas, and I hear my youngest son upstairs playing "Amazing Grace" on his saxophone. My heart is full, and my soul is well. I am so incredibly blessed, and I praise Him for eyes to see it.

I am not saying I will never enjoy another exotic trip because I have everything I need here. But I am saying it is vital to enjoy everyday life with the most important people in your world. I am saying to be content where you are, make amazing memories with those who matter, and make sure they know they matter to you. I know God has so much more for me and mine, and yet I love being here in this moment with Him, with them. Did I mention my youngest then came down and danced in the kitchen with me? Together, we sang, "I love you. Yes, I do. Joshua Caleb . . . how I love you."

I choose to focus on what I do have versus what I don't have. I choose to give gratitude for this day and these people. I breathe in His peace and His rest. Brand this moment and this feeling on my heart and mind for days to come when busy and full throttle emerge again.

I will continue to make SMART goals around my priorities and hold myself accountable to my action steps. I will continue to create a vision board with my dreams from Him and trust Him to help me dream BIGGER and GREATER, knowing HE IS ABLE to fulfill these desires in my heart and life. I will continue to cross the fine line between disciplined/self-control and trying to control things. (I require lots of Jesus in this; at least I admit and recognize it. That is the first step, right?)

Likewise, I will also receive His amazing grace to live fully in the moment and trusting Him with our future . . . one filled with hope and His Promises, that He IS ALWAYS faithful to fulfill.

Now may God, the inspiration and fountain of hope, fill you to overflowing with uncontainable joy and perfect peace as you trust in him. And may the power of the Holy Spirit continually surround your life with his super-abundance until you radiate with hope! (Rom. 15:13)

The Lord your God in your midst, the Mighty One, will save; He will rejoice over you with gladness, He will quiet you with His love, He will rejoice over you with singing." (Zeph. 3:17)

Trust in the Lord, and do good; Dwell in the land, and feed on His faithfulness. 4 Delight yourself also in the Lord, And He shall give you the desires of your heart. (Ps. 37:3–4)

Questions:

1. What are some of your favorite memories? What makes them your favorite?

2. List five daily blessings from this week. How do the blessings reflect the people who mean the most to you?

3. What does your perfect day look like? How can you make most days more closely resemble your BEST DAY EVER?

Sharing What He Has Done in Our Lives

> Raise it up, Fill the sky
> Chains will fall, Mountains move,
> We lift Him high ...
> Strongholds are broken
> I've been made free
> I am forgiven
> Fear has to leave.
>
> —Koryn Hawthorne, "Speak the Name"

At Thanksgiving, we were on the back patio with blankets and coffee. Several of the adults were trying to keep my eighteen-month-old niece out of the mud. The more we told her "no, no," the more she gravitated toward the black mud in her bare feet. She would look at us, daring us to stop her, and then inch closer to the muddy abyss—until finally, she stepped into it with both feet.

Then she began to cry because she did not like the way the mud felt in between her toes. (Same, girl, same. Complete side note: recently, I was invited to participate in a mud run. Do you people know me?) She stood there and cried big crocodile tears until Mommy swept her up in her arms and brought her back onto the porch. Daddy ran in for some wet paper towels to clean off her feet until they were ready to hit the ground running again.

This is a call to all the spiritual moms and dads in the body of Christ. How often do we see the mud that some of our fellow Christians are about to head straight into with both feet? Do we know how to counsel wisdom in love to those around us to help them keep their feet clean? And then are we willing to wash their feet, wipe their tears, and stand them back on their feet again when they find themselves in the place that Holy Spirit and the rest of us told them not to go?

Are we building relationships with people of different cultures, demographics, and tenure in the body of Christ so that when they are in need, they would be willing to receive some wisdom from us? Are we delivering it in a manner that they can receive from us? Are we calling them up versus just calling them out? Do we know how to create influence versus just being right?

Are we willing to be inconvenienced and put ourselves out there in the uncomfortable zone to help people in their journey with Christ? Are we filling ourselves up on the things of God so we can pour back out when others need a fresh word in due season? Are we practicing the Presence of God so we can hear Him when He says, "Text or call this person some encouragement," "Give this person a hug," "Buy this person's lunch"?

I was at a place where I felt like I didn't fit in with our church crowd because many of them are ten or more years younger than me. However, I have realized that many of them can grow from my experiences and counsel. Likewise, I learn and grow from their passion and zeal for Jesus—before life, responsibilities, and hurts. We both have much to offer if we are both open to build authentic relationships, sharing wisdom, and receiving feedback to help us all grow to reach our maximum potential.

I don't need a theology degree and ten years of serving on the church leadership team to share what God has done in my life. I can share how Jesus set me free from a toxic relationship and how He restored my purpose and vision. He fills my cup with my identity in Him. I seek Him first, and I find great joy in loving and serving others. I can share the reward of obedience and sometimes just being in Him. I can also share some consequences from my past of being Jonah—running from my calling in disobedience.

I can share how I learned to leave the past in the past and reach forward to what He has for me in running this race with Him and in

Him. I can share the value of thanksgiving and BELIEVING God for BIG things because I have seen Him do it time and time again.

I pray today you find one person in your church or workplace that you can mentor. I pray you choose to allow Him to grow you into a place you are able to mentor others. Love those around you. Share what He has done in your life. Share the ups and downs and all-arounds to let people know you are real and you are for them. They can trust you to be a safe place to grow on this journey!

> *But whoever has this world's goods, and sees his brother in need, and shuts up his heart from him, how does the love of God abide in him?* (1 John 3:17)

> *Let each of you look out not only for his own interests, but also for the interests of others.* (Phil. 2:4)

> *And the King will answer and say to them, "Assuredly, I say to you, inasmuch as you did it to one of the least of these My brethren, you did it to Me."* (Matt. 25:40)

Questions:

1. Have you been headed in the wrong direction in some areas of your life? How can you listen and respond to the voices around you?

2. Do you see others around you headed into the mud? How can you be a voice of influence in their lives and help restore them?

3. Where can you share your story to make a difference in someone else's life?

So Thankful—The Right Perspective

> More than I could hope or dream of
> You have poured your favor on me
> One day in the house of God is
> Better than a thousand days in the world
> So blessed, I can't contain it
> So much, I've got to give it away
> Your love taught me to live now
> You are more than enough for me.
>
> —Hillsong, "One Day"

I remember arriving in Brazil after thirteen hours on a flight. Sleep deprivation is not a strength for me. I was also in a challenging year, so I was already riding on the struggle bus. We arrived at our hotel, and I just wanted a nap. I knew I was at the edge of me, and I needed a timeout before going out to minister and love on the people.

Due to a miscommunication, our rooms would not be ready for a few hours. I knew I was a ticking time bomb, and I needed to move. I added some caffeine and hit the streets for a long, hard walk. I was complaining and calling it prayer. I was frustrated with myself because I knew all of my emotions were on my face, and I did not look like the leader and ambassador I was supposed to be. I was in the middle of asking God why He had sent me here because I was not in my best headspace to give out to His people. He was asking too much. Other people take sabbaticals, why can't I? Blah, blah, blah.

I walked past a homeless man, who was eating rice off the sidewalk from the dumpster, and it slammed into me like a ton of bricks. What was wrong with me? I am so ridiculously blessed, and I am whining over a lack of sleep. I have the incredible opportunity to be in multiple nations to share His love and encouragement. Does it REALLY matter that I am not at peak performance level? Suck it up, buttercup. Choose to be grateful. Go where He sends you and give what you have. It is still so much more than what many of these people have ever seen.

Because I chose to be thankful, prostitutes found Jesus. Because I decided to keep moving when I wanted to lie down, impoverished children received Jesus and food. Because I said yes when I wanted to say no, single moms received a word of encouragement. Because I gave what I had, struggling ministries received a miracle. Because of Him in me, even in some of my weakest moments, I was completely undone and unraveled in a way that He could use me.

I pray you choose to be thankful during this season. Praise Him for your health. Praise Him for your children. Praise Him for the roof over your head. Praise Him for your job. Praise Him for your community. Praise Him for your church. Praise Him for a nation where you can freely worship Jesus. Praise Him because of the Cross. If HE never did anything else for you (and of course, He WILL), this was MORE THAN ENOUGH.

> *In everything, give thanks: for this is the will of God in Christ Jesus concerning you.* (1 Thess. 5:18)

> *Be anxious for nothing, but in everything by prayer and supplication, with thanksgiving, let your requests be made known to God;* [7] *and the peace of God, which surpasses all understanding, will guard your hearts and minds through Christ Jesus.* (Phil. 4:6)

> *Oh give thanks unto the LORD, for HE IS good: for His mercy endures forever.* (Ps. 107:1)

Questions:

1. Have you ever found you were at the end of your rope? How did you respond under pressure? What are some steps you can take to better respond in the future?

2. Have you ever found yourself being ungrateful for the many blessings in your life? Every morning, I start my day off with five things I am thankful for from the previous day. List five things you are thankful for today.

3. What are some ways you can serve and help those less fortunate than you?

4. Have you ever not felt like serving? Felt like not doing what God has asked you to do? What do you do to lay down your feelings and do the right thing?

Take a Moment

> Then I hear You say,
> "You don't have to do a thing
> Simply be with Me and let those things go
> They can wait another minute
> Wait, this moment is too sweet
> Please stay here with me
> And love on Me a little longer."
>
> —Jenn Johnson, "A Little Longer"

I was heading home from a soccer game, and I looked at my gas tank to see that I had twenty-three miles left until empty. As someone who fills up the tank when it is at the halfway mark, it made me realize the hectic pace of my weekend. Five soccer games, two birthday parties, two workouts, and one emergency room visit. (I am raising boys, don't judge, something about a football, grate, and drumsticks. Sigh.)

I think about how often we go through our days running from one thing to the next, completely emptying our tanks. Then we try to continue to give out on fumes so that those that are most important to us may not get our best versions of ourselves.

The Martha and Mary story always brings an internal dialogue, maybe even a debate on the inside of me. Steven Furtick once talked about how Martha had a job. She paid the bills. I take that a step further. I think maybe if Mary had helped, then they would have been finished in half the time. Both could have then sat at the feet of Jesus.

People often tell me I should have more fun. Sometimes I am like Martha, and I want to say, really? I am a single mom raising two boys. I am a senior-level executive working forty to fifty hours a week to provide for them. I just finished my MBA, so I am always in a position to provide for them. Someone has to be the responsible one, and guess what, that fell on my shoulders whether I asked for it or not. So fun—finishing a workout that helps me with my sanity ... is FUN.

Having money left over after paying the bills is also really FUN. Having all calls, emails, and texts for work completely caught up is completely FUN.

Then Holy Spirit is like, "Down, Simba, go stand in the corner and breathe." Jesus said Mary had chosen the right thing. At that moment, she chose to sit at the feet of Jesus. Sometimes we have to know when to turn aside like Moses did to see and hear God in the burning bush. Sometimes we have to turn off social media and the other noise to hear Him more clearly. Sometimes we have to stop the hectic routine to see the hurting person next to us who may need a smile, a word of encouragement, or a meal.

Sometimes I just hear Him say, "Come away with Me. Let Me show you great and mighty things you do not know." Sometimes I have to unplug from everything else and just plug into Him.

I pray today that you take that necessary time to sit at the feet of Jesus to hear Him and know Him more. Lay down the responsibilities for a few moments and trust Him to multiply your time back to you. He IS faithful to redeem the time.

> *38-39 As Jesus and the disciples continued on their journey, they came to a village where a woman welcomed Jesus into her home. Her name was Martha and she had a sister named Mary. Mary sat down attentively before the Master, absorbing every revelation he shared. 40 But Martha became exasperated by finishing the numerous household chores in preparation for her guests, so she interrupted Jesus and said, "Lord, don't you think it's unfair that my sister left me to do all the work by myself? You should tell her to get up and help me."*

⁴¹ The Lord answered her, "Martha, my beloved Martha. Why are you upset and troubled, pulled away by all these many distractions? Are they really that important? ⁴² Mary has discovered the one thing most important by choosing to sit at my feet. She is undistracted, and I won't take this privilege from her." (Luke 10:39–42)

Questions:

1. Do you see yourself as more of a Mary or a Martha? How can you have more Mary moments in your life? If you are a Mary, do you see some places you could be a Martha?

2. How can you have better quality and quantity of time at the feet of Jesus?

3. Since the JOY of the LORD is your strength, what are some ways you can infuse your day with more joy?

Take One Step

> I'm takin' a step of faith
> Walkin' out on the promises God made
> Takin' a giant leap in the air
> Steppin' out on nothin' and findin' somethin' there
> Tellin' the doubt to wait
> I'm takin' a step of faith
> Living for the LORD, trusting in His care
> Steppin' out on nothin' and findin' somethin' there.
>
> —Carmen, "Step of Faith"

I remember sitting at my desk in my quiet time studying John 5:2–9 about the paralytic at the pool of Bethesda. The man had waited thirty-eight years. He had watched others receive their miracle in his place, and yet he waited . . . unfulfilled.

Honestly, I was snarky in my head for a moment. I thought, *I would have rolled into that pool. I would have demonstrated determination and perseverance . . . nothing holding me back from my miracle."*

Immediately, Holy Spirit convicted me. He said, "Don't judge what you do not know. Did you ever walk in his shoes? Do you know what was in his heart?" I immediately repented, and I began to ask, "What is that one step of faith that I need to take to move my family and me into that next place You have called us?"

Before I could finish the thought, I clearly heard Him say, "Pack your bags and move to Royse City." Slam the brakes. Slow down. WHAT? I began to push back. (You may see a pattern here). "Wait a minute. This is not in the plan or budget. The spreadsheet has us ready to go in 2–3 years."

"Now is the time. Do not miss it. Partial obedience in your time is not the same as complete obedience in My time. Take that one step of faith and trust Me to do the rest." Sigh.

So I called my realtor friend and asked her to put my house on the market. We started packing, as though it was already time. I connected with another realtor to look for houses in the Royse City market. I called my mentors and asked them to pray and share any wisdom.

Within three weeks, we sold and bought a house. My house was never even on the market, as we received a cash purchase. God transitioned my job and raised my salary to absorb extra expenses. It was a complete whirlwind, and yet God supplied our every need and many desires.

Like the Apostle Paul in his travels, he moved in a direction, and often the Holy Spirit would redirect his steps. Like Joseph, when he was ready to walk away from Mary, an angel visited and redirected his steps. Sometimes it is easier for God to alter our course when we are already in motion versus paralysis of analysis.

My prayer is that you would be completely obedient in this moment to all He has asked you to do. Sometimes you have to take one step into the River Jordan before He splits the sea to allow you to walk on dry land to the other side. One step is all it takes. May He prosper everything you put your hand (and step) to exceedingly and abundantly above anything you could ever ask for, think of, or even imagine. He makes the way where there seems to be no way, and He makes the crooked paths straight. He goes before you and prepares the way.

> *Now faith is the substance of things hoped for, the evidence of things not seen.* (Heb. 11:1)

> *But without faith it is impossible to please Him, for he who comes to God must believe that He is, and that He is a rewarder of those who diligently seek Him. 7 By faith Noah, being divinely warned of things not yet seen, moved with*

godly fear, prepared an ark for the saving of his household, by which he condemned the world and became heir of the righteousness which is according to faith. 8 By faith Abraham obeyed when he was called to go out to the place which he would receive as an inheritance. And he went out, not knowing where he was going. (Heb. 11:6–8)

Questions:

1. Have you judged someone or a situation before understanding what it is like to walk in their shoes? How can you step back in grace to pray for them and encourage them?

2. Stop and ask what is that next step you can take to better position you and your family to do all that He has called you to do. How will you hold yourself accountable to take that step of faith?

3. What's the one miracle you are asking for today? How can you put your faith, the size of a mustard seed, out there to move your mountain?

The Faith of a Child

Draw me close to you, Never let me go
I lay it all down again
To hear you say that I'm your friend
You are my desire, No one else will do
'Cause nothing else can take your place
To feel the warmth of your embrace
Help me find the way, Bring me back to you

—Michael W. Smith, "Draw Me Close to You"

My youngest son sold his virtual reality headset online (actually, Mrs. Miriam sold it for him), and he already had the money spent toward an upgraded headset before the funds had even materialized. Mrs. Miriam explained to him that it took a week to complete the sales and purchase process before actual cash hits our account. AND she reminded him that I had not agreed to purchase the upgrade for Christmas—that was still a month away. He informed her that he believed in miracles. "The money will be there. Mom will agree. Let's go ahead and purchase the new headset."

Mrs. Miriam said to me, "Your children know that you always take care of them. It's just an expectation. You have never let them down." She paused in that moment and let the silence speak volumes. "God wants you to have that same expectation and trust in Him that He has you in this situation. He will take care of you. He already has the answer, and it is going to be SOOOO GOOD."

Isn't it interesting that our children KNOW and TRUST us? I can remember driving home in a torrential downpour from a soccer game that cancelled the minute we drove into the parking lot of the stadium over an hour away . . . GRRRRR. My visibility on the road was almost nonexistent, and it was only supposed to get worse. As I was praying for safety and wisdom, I noticed the same youngest son sound asleep in the backseat. He was not concerned as to whether or not we would make it home safely. He was not even aware of the dangers surrounding us. He just knew that Mom and Jesus always took care of him.

I sat down and thought through the stones of remembrance of all the places He has provided made the way where there seemed to be no way and divinely intervened in our lives. I remember when He used people to drop checks in the mail to help pay our bills. People would bring bags of barely used clothes so the boys never went without nice clothing. I remember Him delivering us from chaos and a life-threatening situation into safety and peace.

I remember unexpected bonuses, 8 percent raises when everyone else was receiving 2 percent and 3 percent increases. I experienced promotions, income tax checks, random checks in the mail—always more than enough to take care of us. I remember fully and/or partially paid work trips for the boys and me to Costa Rica and other exotic places that we could never afford on our own. I remember us posting our dreams on vision boards and then praying God's Word to see those things come to pass in our lives. Over and over again, He MORE than answered our prayers.

So WHY IS IT that every time we face a seemingly insurmountable challenge we start wondering whether or not He WILL take care of us this time? I used to read about the Israelites wandering around the desert for forty years for what should have been a twelve- to thirteen-day trip. I would think how ridiculous they were. Now I realize I have been going around this mountain of will He take care of us, will He do it again, did He bring us this far to drop us now for forty-five years. AND here I am again.

When the Israelites painted the blood of the lamb over the doorposts of their homes to protect their firstborn sons as the angel of death swept through the night, they could stay up all night and worry or they could trust that the blood of the lamb would protect them.

I can worry and be anxious, or I can have the faith of a child. I can trust that He will take care of us, just as He ALWAYS has. I can know that the blood of the lamb is over my home and everything that pertains to me and mine. I can fully expect that goodness and blessings from God will pour out over our hearts and lives. I can know that He loves us, and He IS for us.

I pray today that you can hand over whatever is bothering you into the hands of God Almighty. You can know and trust that He will take care of every detail. You can know and fully expect that He has this situation under control. He will not leave you. He will not let you go. He will see you through to the other side of this, and it will be SOOOO GOOD.

> *Be anxious for nothing, but in everything by prayer and supplication, with thanksgiving, let your requests be made known to God; 7 and the peace of God, which surpasses all understanding, will guard your hearts and minds through Christ Jesus. 8 Finally, brethren, whatever things are true, whatever things are noble, whatever things are just, whatever things are pure, whatever things are lovely, whatever things are of good report, if there is any virtue and if there is anything praiseworthy—meditate on these things. 9 The things which you learned and received and heard and saw in me, these do, and the God of peace will be with you. (Phil. 4:6–9)*

Questions:

1. What areas of your life do you place more faith in Amazon Prime (or the mail service) than you do in Jesus fulfilling the Promises He has given you? How can you switch this paradigm?

2. What are places where you believed BIG for an answer from God, and He delivered? What are the places now that you have before Him?

3. List your top five worries. How can you hand these over to God and release faith over each of these situations?

The Great Exchange

> Beautiful rations
> And joy for my pain
> He turns weeping into dancing
> every time I praise
> Burdens are lifting
> Doubts begin to cease
> He removes the heavy burden
> And brings the sweetest peace.
>
> —Martha Munizzi, "Great Exchange"

I woke up one morning to make coffee in my new cup from Australia (a gift from a friend of mine who had attended the Hillsong worship conference). I saw it dirty in the sink from someone who had exploded cocoa all over the cup, counter, and microwave the evening before. Sigh, pick a different country.

As a mom, my boys (and my dog) have this mentality that whatever is mine is theirs—and whatever is theirs is theirs. From my white duvet cover (now shredded) to my white bathroom towels (used for bloody noses), from my preworkout drinks and protein bars (it's healthier than a candy bar, not if you eat three a day) to my desk in my office (I like yours better; yes, me too), they have a habit of taking over my stuff, time, and resources.

Yesterday, I was powering through a migraine and then not powering through so great. I was irritated to lose valuable writing time and a workout. (I had fasted exercise the previous day, and two days in a row DO NOT HAPPEN.) Then I shifted my mindset and realized that my fourteen-year-old was hanging out with me. He had crawled up beside me on my bed, and he was sharing funny videos (very quietly out of respect for my head).

Then after he left, my twelve-year-old came and started talking to me about eating crickets at camp—it's a long story. I thought about Steve Jobs's last words about valuing family and friends over all of his crazy success as a billionaire—only to die and lose it all at fifty-six from pancreatic cancer. And I thought I would exchange memories and moments with my boys any day over a workout. As much as I love writing to you and ministering to you, I still choose laughing with them first.

Then I think of the great exchange. Inconveniently (understatement of eternity), Jesus died on the Cross, and what was His became ours. He gave us righteousness for our filthy sin. He gave us His abundance for our lack. He gave us health in place of sickness. He gave us hope in place of disappointment and discouragement. I am so grateful that He was willing to brutally shed His blood so that He could reconcile you and me back to Him.

Broken windows from soccer balls, lost hoodies, broken lamps from chasing the horse-sized dog through my house aren't my favorite, would just like a few things to stay nice. Sigh, but I am thankful for the exchange of good memories and relationships with my boys that will always remain.

I pray today that we would never take the Great Exchange for granted. Live out the fullness of everything He has for you because He paid an extravagant price for you. Likewise, enjoy the wins with family and friends—even when it is inconvenient and costly. Life passes quickly. Know what matters, and make what matters known.

> *The thief does not come except to steal, and to kill, and to destroy. I have come that they may have life, and that they may have it more abundantly.* (John 10:10)

For you know the grace of our Lord Jesus Christ, that though He was rich, yet for your sakes He became poor, that you through His poverty might become rich. (2 Cor. 8:9)

Who Himself bore our sins in His own body on the tree, that we, having died to sins, might live for righteousness—by whose stripes you were healed. (1 Pet. 2:24)

Questions:

1. What people and situations do you see as inconvenient or frustrating versus seeing them the way God sees them? How can you change your perspective?

2. Have you embraced the GREAT EXCHANGE of the Cross from Jesus Christ? What does this look like in your life?

3. What things can you give Him (anxiety, worry, negativity, insecurity) in exchange for His Best (peace, Promises, encouragement, confidence)?

The Power of Listening

When sorrows roar and troubles rage
You whisper peace when I don't have the words to say
I won't lose hope when storms won't break
You keep Your word, oh and Your promises will keep me safe

I don't wanna miss one word You speak
'Cause everything You say is life to me
I don't wanna miss one word You speak
So quiet my heart, I'm listening.

—Chris McClarney, "I'm Listening"

Recently, my boss gave me some valuable advice: "Don't go into this conversation to debate or justify. Truly, just listen. Accept what she says, and thank her for the feedback." Part of me wanted to argue that I was great at listening, and Holy Spirit immediately showed me a conversation from the previous evening, where I had not listened so well and explained myself—just like he warned against. Uggggh.

Then we were all on a phone call with a potential partnership, and I heard the sales guy talk for nine minutes straight without asking what we wanted from this partnership. He did not inquire as to why we had requested the call. He rambled about everything except why we had requested the call without even taking a breath. It made me laugh, especially in light of the recent conversations about my shortcomings.

How often do we miss valuable feedback or insight into others because we are forming our next sentence and thought without really listening to what someone has to say? How often do we silence those around us by talking over them? How often do we diminish the value of a friend or colleague's thoughts or opinions by finishing the sentence or inserting our response—or worse, a completely different thought strand?

Listening to music pushes me through a workout, brings back great memories around the holidays, or can even push me through a difficult season with some great worship.

Hearing my children's laughter echo throughout the house always brings a smile to my face.

Listening to a funny video with them or one of their jokes makes me laugh out loud with them. Hearing their footsteps near my door wakes me out of the deepest sleep so I can make sure everything is well with them. Sometimes their body language or tone speaks volumes—even more than their words.

Listening in communication allows us to build better relationships, better understand people in our lives, better identify solutions to situations, and establish trust and credibility. Whether it's networking and building new relationships, interviews, negotiations, or mediation, it is imperative that I listen to everything that is said—and not said.

Knowing all these things about listening, how often are we still in the Presence of God to hear Him? He is always talking. Prayer has to be a two-way communication street. I come to Him with thanksgiving and praise in my heart. I pray for those around me. I read His Word and apply it to my life today. I ask Him.

And then I wait. I wait for what He will whisper into my heart. I write it down, and I continue to pray over it until I see it come to pass in our lives.

Sometimes He drops a name on my heart. I hear Him and respond by texting, calling, and praying for that person. At other times, I hear specific instructions for someone or an encouraging word, and then I obey. I may hear or sense a deeper revelation of a Scripture that becomes incredibly important to me in a season. He also has others reach out to me with confirmation or encouragement of things He is doing in my life. Again, I sit and listen. Once I have peace about a situation, then I can move forward.

I pray today that you would have ears to hear. Open your hearts and minds to what He IS saying to you throughout the day. He will guide your footsteps and use you to be a blessing to someone around you. I pray you would quiet your mind and position yourself to hear His counsel and encouragement for you today. He loves you with an everlasting love, and He loves to lead you in all things if you just listen and obey. Your life will never be the same.

> *Wherefore, my beloved brethren, let every man be swift to hear, slow to speak, slow to wrath.* (James 1:19)

> *So Moses said, "I must turn aside now and see this marvelous sight, why the bush is not burned up." 4 When the Lord saw that he turned aside to look, God called to him from the midst of the bush and said, "Moses, Moses!" And he said, "Here I am."* (Exod. 3:3–4)

> *Your ears shall hear a word behind you, saying, "This is the way, walk in it," Whenever you turn to the right hand or whenever you turn to the left.* (Isa. 30:21)

> *My sheep hear my voice, and I know them, and they follow Me.* (John 10:27)

Questions:

1. What is the most valuable advice you have recently received? How do you apply this to your life?

2. Think of the past three conversations you have had. How well did you listen? Give examples that illustrate you listened well. How can you improve your listening skills in relationships and communication?

3. Are you willing to receive feedback from others in your life? What does this look like, and how do you use feedback from others to continually improve your walk with God and your overall life?

Wisdom to Make Great Choices

I've been strong, and I've been broken within a moment
I've been faithful, and I've been reckless at every bend
I've held everything together and watched it shatter
I've stood tall, and I have crumbled in the same breath

I have wrestled, and I have trembled toward surrender
Chased my heart adrift and drifted home again
Plundered blessing till I've been desperate to find redemption
And every time I turn around Lord, You're still there

—Hillsong UNITED, "As You Find Me"

A friend and I were hiking the Katy Trail in Dallas. Okay, actually we were walking while pretending we were wilderness explorers in downtown/uptown Dallas. It's a similar experience, I'm sure. As I was sharing some life experiences and lessons learned, she said it made her feel better to know that I could make my not-so-best decisions sometimes too.

I always laugh when people presume that we get to this place in life that we don't make a wrong decision or have an off moment. My youngest son was riding shotgun on the way to church, and he said, "Mom, I don't think you ever make mistakes. You make the best decisions." Outwardly, I laughed. Inwardly, I cringed. "Joshua, I would love to let you think I always make great decisions, but the reality is we are always one decision away from our best life and one decision away from a mess."

We make choices all day that agree with the Spirit of God on the inside of us, or we agree with our flesh. A few decisions in either direction can make or break us for the moment. David was a man after

God's own heart; however, he committed adultery with Bathsheba and murdered her husband, Uriah.

God says wisdom is available for the asking. The more we read His Word and spend time with Him in the quiet place, the more wisdom we exhibit to experience good choices flowing through us. He also says His mercies are new every day because we generally need them every day.

On one hand, stay so close to the voice and Presence of God that you walk out of that Scripture having the mind of Christ. David would ask for God's wisdom before the various battles. He would ask if the LORD would hand over the enemies. When the LORD said yes, he would pursue and take the enemy. Invite the Holy Spirit into your daily decisions. He will guide you through each one of them. He is intentional and cares about anything that pertains to you.

On the other hand, there is forgiveness when you blow it. Repent, do a 180-degree heart turn, and keep moving with Christ. You are the righteousness of God in Christ Jesus, and He will order your steps. Keep reaching forward and forget those things that are behind you.

Don't be afraid to share the places you fell and skinned your knees. Those words may be exactly what someone needs to be delivered and set free from the chains that are holding them back. If God did it for you, someone can now have the faith that He will do it for them.

I pray you would abide in Christ, listen to His voice, and obey. I pray you would ask for and walk in His wisdom. I pray you would receive forgiveness and mercy on a regular basis. I pray you would keep running hard after the things of God, get back up when you fall down, and don't ever stop running this race.

> *Get wisdom! Get understanding! Do not forget, nor turn away from the words of my mouth. 6 Do not forsake her, and she will preserve you; Love her, and she will keep you. 7 Wisdom is the principal thing; Therefore, get wisdom. And in all your getting, get understanding. 8 Exalt her, and she will promote you; She will bring you honor, when you embrace her. 9 She will place on your head an ornament of grace; A crown of glory she will deliver to you. (Prov. 4:5–9)*

Questions:

1. What are the three best decisions you have made over the past year that clearly demonstrates God's wisdom in your life? What are the three worst decisions that showed some areas of opportunity for growth in your life?

2. What areas of your life have you submitted to God and asked Him for wisdom and guidance?

3. Who do you have in your life as a mentor or person that you submit to for wisdom and counsel?

You Are My Hiding Place

You are my hiding place
You always fill my heart
With songs of deliverance
Whenever I am afraid
I will trust in You.

—Selah, "You Are My Hiding Place"

It's one of those nights when sleep eludes me. I can allow the fear and worry to continue circulating through my mind, or I can come away to the secret place and fix my eyes and heart on God. Once again, my humanity hits me head-on, and I need to hear His voice.

I come into His Presence with thanksgiving in my heart and praise on my lips. I am thankful for my amazing boys, who are healthy, whole, and fabulous. I am thankful to be in great health. I am grateful for the many wonderful friends and family who surround me. I am thankful to live in a country where I can freely worship Jesus, and the most persecution I receive is somebody's hateful words.

I praise Him because I know He IS Faithful. I praise Him because He IS Worthy. I praise Him because He loves me and mine. I praise Him even in this moment that I cannot see, hear, or understand. He knows. He cares. He IS already acting on my behalf. The weapon may form against me, but it shall not prosper. He makes a table for me in the midst of my enemies. He anoints my head. My cup runs over. Surely goodness and mercy will follow me all the days of my life, and we will dwell in the House of the LORD forever. I praise Him because He IS my Father. He IS the lifter of my head. I rise and shine because the glory of God is upon me.

I talk to Him like He IS my Best Friend—because He IS. I lay my burden down at His feet. I was never created to carry this. His burden is light, and His yoke is easy. I tell Him my day, week, month, and most of this year has not gone exactly the way I thought it would. And I tell Him that it has been exceptionally hard, and I am really tired—tired of being strong, tired of not being strong enough, tired of fighting, tired of waiting, tired of seeing breakthrough in the distance, but not in this place. Tired.

I tell Him I am scared about the future because I don't know what it holds. I am scared of not being able to provide for my boys, scared of letting people around me down, scared of being this mighty warrior crumbling to her knees, scared of allowing the tears to fall, scared that if I soften just a bit, I might break. Scared of unraveling... scared.

He says, "Come under the shadow of My wings, and let Me give you rest. Lay it all down in complete surrender, that I may pick it up for you. I AM your Refuge and Strong Tower. I AM your Vindicator, and you can trust Me. I AM for you, who can be against you? I have made you the head and not the tail, above and not beneath, MORE than a conqueror in ME. You are an overcomer, and this will not overtake you. You are a tree planted by the waters with roots that go wide and deep. You will bear fruit when others are drying up around you. You have nothing to fear but fear itself. I love you with an everlasting love. Let Me love you in this place of fear—any place you feel fear or worry is simply a place where you have not allowed Me to love you. Let go, and just let Me love you."

I choose to let His love wash over me. I choose to enter those streams of refreshing. I choose Him, His Promises, His Love. I choose to rewrite the script moving through my mind. I choose to believe Him when He says He is already fighting on my behalf. I choose to believe He loves my boys even more than me, which is so hard to comprehend. I choose to believe He loves me that much too. I choose to trust in what I cannot see, feel, touch, hear. I choose to let Him love me. I choose.

I pray that you would let Him love you today. He sees. He cares. He knows, and He loves you more than you will ever even begin to understand—just because you are His. I pray you stop wrestling with the future that does not even exist. I pray you would be still and know that He IS God. Know that He IS for you. He cannot fail, as He IS a God Who always triumphs. And because you are in HIM, you will overcome as a victor. Fear not, He IS WITH YOU. He will never leave you nor forsake you.

> *Say to those who are fearful-hearted, "Be strong, do not fear! Behold, your God will come with vengeance, With the recompense of God; He will come and save you." (Isa. 35:4)*

> *Peace I leave with you, My peace I give to you; not as the world gives do I give to you. Let not your heart be troubled, neither let it be afraid. (John 14:27)*

> *Have I not commanded you? Be strong and of good courage; do not be afraid, nor be dismayed, for the Lord your God is with you wherever you go. (Josh. 1:9)*

Questions:

1. Do you have difficulty sleeping at night or controlling the thoughts in your mind that lead to worry, anxiety, depression, anger? What behaviors can you change to take captive your thoughts and emotions?

2. What are the situations in your life that bring fear or worry? How can you submit those circumstances to God and let Him take care of you and yours?

3. How can you practice resting and being still to know that He IS GOD?

You Are So Loved

> And we are His portion, and He is our prize
> Drawn to redemption by the grace in His eyes
> If grace is an ocean, we're all sinking
> So Heaven meets earth like an unforeseen kiss
> And my heart turns violently inside of my chest
> I don't have time to maintain these regrets
> When I think about the way . . . He loves us, Oh, how He loves us . . . How He loves us so.
>
> —David Crowder, "How He Loves"

Someone once told me that anywhere I face fear or mistrust is a place I haven't allowed God to love me, that I needed a revelation of His GREAT love for me because His perfect love casts out all fear.

Isaiah 49:23 tells us that those who hope in Him will never be disappointed. First Peter 2:6 says that those who trust in the LORD will never be disappointed. The dictionary defines *disappointed* as "sad or displeased because someone or something has failed to fulfill one's hopes or expectations." The Word also tells us that hope deferred makes the heart sick.

I remember this life-changing conversation with the LORD: "But I do get disappointed—in fact, I have spent much of this year being disappointed." He gently whispered, "Then you don't trust Me." "NO, Lord, of course, I trust YOU. I am just frustrated and disappointed that it takes so long to see the answers that I have been praying and believing for over these last years. I am so thankful for the many blessings in our lives. I just know YOU could move in these other areas, and I don't understand why the answer has been no, or not now."

Again, the whisper: "Then you really don't trust Me. You don't trust that I love you with a love so great, so wide, so deep, so all-encompassing. You don't trust that My love always and intentionally has your best interest in mind. You don't fully trust Me to do this for you and fight these battles on your behalf. You don't trust that My love is bigger than your worthiness, bigger than your failures, bigger than your circumstances. I see your end from your beginning, and I am working all things together for your good—like weaving a tapestry with the end result already known and seen before the first threads are interlaced. You don't believe that My love is for you in all things—not really."

It was a sobering and profound moment to realize I still had closed-off places to His love because I couldn't handle the hurt if He really didn't come through, if He really didn't answer my prayers. Bill Johnson once said, "Don't water down the Word to match your circumstances, but elevate your circumstances to match His Promises in His Word."

He ALWAYS answers. It may not look the way we thought it would, and rarely does it happen in the timeline we have created in our minds. People around us have choices, and there are both good times and bad due to sin and the fallenness of the world around us. But God—HE IS FAITHFUL. He loves us so much that He gave His only begotten Son that we could be redeemed and restored into this lavish love relationships with Him. He sings over us even when we sleep, as a mother does over her sleeping babe. He placed dreams on the inside of us, and He WILL give us the desires of our hearts in a way that far surpasses our human expectations.

I pray you are still in the quiet place today and allow Him to fully love you—to give you a revelation of how deeply loved and valuable you are to Him. I pray you would open your heart again to receive His love and all He has for you. May you walk in strength and dignity and laugh without fear of the future.

And we have known and believed the love that God has for us. God is love, and he who abides in love abides in God, and God in him. (1 John 4:16)

Our fathers trusted in You; They trusted, and You delivered them. 5 They cried to You, and were delivered; They trusted in You, and were not ashamed. (Ps. 22:4–5)

Questions:

1. Where are you experiencing disappointment, discouragement, or fear? How can you receive a revelation of God's never-failing love for you in these areas?

2. Where are the places that you don't trust God to answer your prayers? Do you fully trust Him with the lives of your spouse? Your children? Your finances? Your future? How can you give Him EVERY area of your life in full surrender?

About the Author

Chanda Fulgium is a lifelong lover of Jesus. She has found success in corporate America with faith principles in the health care world with fourteen years in the wound care industry, and she is now the chief strategy officer at Wound Integrity. She holds an MBA and an MS in communication studies.

Likewise, she does leadership and motivational training in the corporate and ministry worlds, both in the United States and around the world. Her mission in life is to release God's potential and launch people into their destinies.

Finally, she is the mother of two of the most amazing boys in the universe, Elijah David (14) and Joshua Caleb (12).

Made in the USA
San Bernardino, CA
27 February 2020